The Green Witch

ILLUSTRATED

An Enchanting Immersion

INTO THE MAGIC OF

NATURAL WITCHCRAFT

ARIN MURPHY-HISCOCK
ILLUSTRATED BY SARA RICHARD

ADAMS MEDIA

NEW YORK   LONDON   TORONTO   SYDNEY   NEW DELHI

Adams Media
An Imprint of Simon & Schuster, LLC
100 Technology Center Drive
Stoughton, Massachusetts 02072

First Adams Media hardcover edition November 2024

ADAMS MEDIA and colophon are registered trademarks of
Simon & Schuster, LLC.

Simon & Schuster: Celebrating 100 Years of Publishing in 2024

For information about special discounts for bulk purchases,
please contact Simon & Schuster Special Sales at 1-866-506-1949
or business@simonandschuster.com.

The Simon & Schuster Speakers Bureau can bring authors to
your live event. For more information or to book an event, contact
the Simon & Schuster Speakers Bureau at 1-866-248-3049 or
visit our website at www.simonspeakers.com.

Interior design by Colleen Cunningham, Priscilla Yuen, and
Frank Rivera
Illustrations by Sara Richard
Background images © Getty Images/CallMeTak, Boonyachoat,
Svetlanais, Djahan; 123RF/KATSUMI MUROUCHI, Natalija
Gagarina

Manufactured in the United States of America

10 9 8 7 6 5 4 3 2 1

Library of Congress Cataloging-in-Publication Data has
been applied for.

ISBN 978-1-5072-2319-2
ISBN 978-1-5072-2320-8 (ebook)

Contains material adapted from the following titles
published by Adams Media, an Imprint of Simon
& Schuster, LLC: *The Green Witch* by Arin Murphy-
Hiscock, copyright © 2017, ISBN 978-1-5072-0471-9,
and *The Green Witch's Garden* by Arin Murphy-
Hiscock, copyright © 2021, ISBN 978-1-5072-1587-6.

EX · LIBRIS

Contents

Introduction

The way of the green witch is the path of the naturalist, the herbalist, and the healer.

They work closely with natural elements to improve the well-being of the body, the spirit, and the environment. If you are looking to deepen your connection with nature, let *The Green Witch Illustrated* be your guide to exploring all the green witch path has to offer. With all new vibrant illustrations and updated material, this volume will take you on a sensory exploration of what it means to be a green witch—and the tools, rituals, and meditations that can help you find the balance you are seeking. The lush illustrations in this book will enhance your practice by helping you see, feel, and understand the connection to nature that all green witches wish to build. Through them you will discover more about the free-form, flexible, and personalized practice of green witchcraft, including a fully illustrated guide to the trees, herbs, flowers, and stones you'll need to know.

You'll also find beautifully and thoughtfully designed pages of recipes, meditations, rituals, and directions for making potions and herbal blends for purposes both mundane and magical.

The Green Witch Illustrated is a positive and practical guide for the modern green witch trying to connect with nature in today's world. Let the vibrant illustrations in this book open your senses and bring you a sense of appreciation for the environment and the harmony it possesses. Through the comprehensive and relatable advice in these pages you will discover how to connect your modern life to that earlier knowledge that is waiting for you to find it again. The secret is to recognize the presence of green energy in the world today and see how it still operates—and this book will show you how.

Listen to the world around you.

Open your heart.

Rebalance.

And enjoy your journey.

CHAPTER 1

WHAT *is* GREEN WITCHCRAFT?

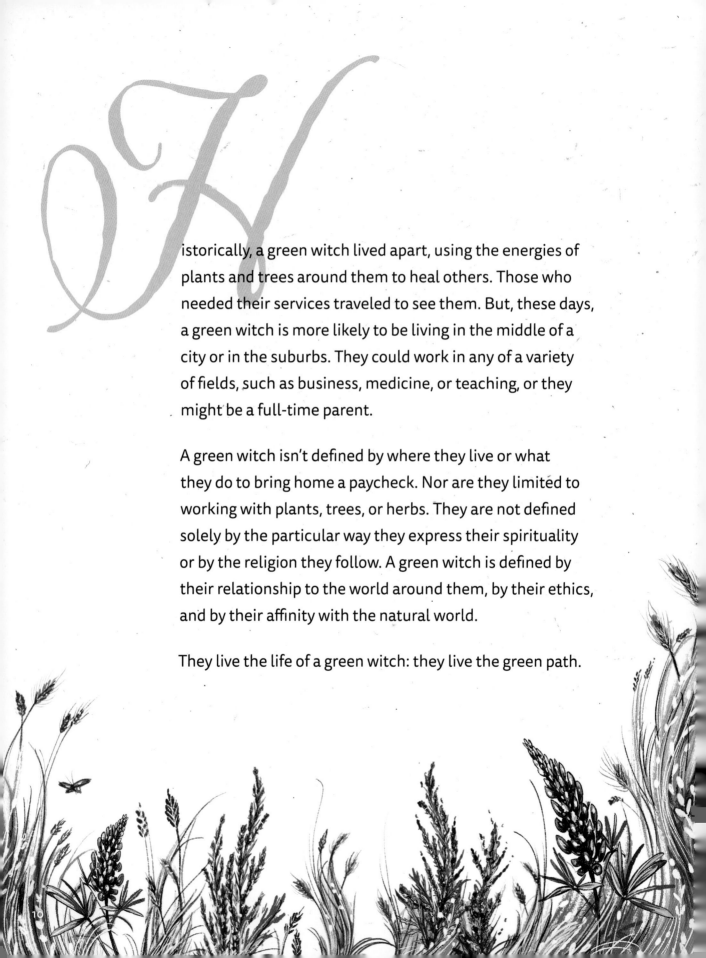

istorically, a green witch lived apart, using the energies of plants and trees around them to heal others. Those who needed their services traveled to see them. But, these days, a green witch is more likely to be living in the middle of a city or in the suburbs. They could work in any of a variety of fields, such as business, medicine, or teaching, or they might be a full-time parent.

A green witch isn't defined by where they live or what they do to bring home a paycheck. Nor are they limited to working with plants, trees, or herbs. They are not defined solely by the particular way they express their spirituality or by the religion they follow. A green witch is defined by their relationship to the world around them, by their ethics, and by their affinity with the natural world.

They live the life of a green witch: they live the green path.

WALK the GREEN WITCH PATH

In popular perception, the practice of green witchcraft is a nature-based expression of spirituality that focuses on the individual's interaction with his or her natural environment. Witchcraft itself is a practice that involves the use of natural energies as an aid to accomplishing a task or reaching a goal. In general, witchcraft acknowledges a god and a goddess (sometimes solely a goddess) and recognizes that magic is a natural phenomenon. For the sake of this book, the term "witchcraft" refers to the practice of working with natural energies to attain goals, without a specific religious context.

A green witch, then, is someone who lives the green path and is aware of how the energy of nature flows through their life and environment, even if that environment is not the traditional garden and forest setting popularized by fairy tales and romanticized notions.

THE PRACTICE

The concepts of healing, harmony, and balance
are all key to the green witch's practice and outlook on life.
These concepts embody three distinct focuses:

❧

Earth

Your local environment, as well as the planet.

❧

Humanity

In general, as well as your local community and
circles of friends and acquaintances.

❧

Yourself

Your true self and the realities of your life.

"We will say

living the path

instead of simply saying

practicing green witchcraft

because green witchcraft is not a

practice separate from ordinary life.

It is an all-encompassing, total-

immersion experience wherein all

of life is a magical experience."

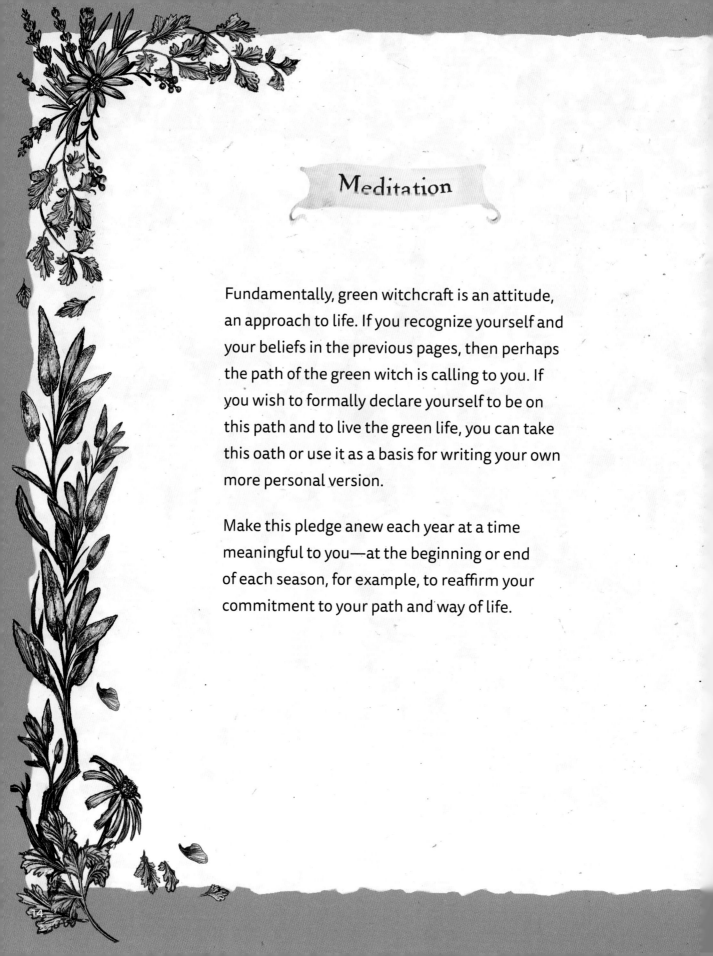

Meditation

Fundamentally, green witchcraft is an attitude, an approach to life. If you recognize yourself and your beliefs in the previous pages, then perhaps the path of the green witch is calling to you. If you wish to formally declare yourself to be on this path and to live the green life, you can take this oath or use it as a basis for writing your own more personal version.

Make this pledge anew each year at a time meaningful to you—at the beginning or end of each season, for example, to reaffirm your commitment to your path and way of life.

OATH OF THE GREEN WITCH

Lord and Lady,
Spirits of Nature,
Elements around me,
Bless me as I walk the path of the green witch.

May my every action be for the good of all,
For Humanity and Nature alike.

Bring me wisdom and peace,
Serenity and balance as I walk this path.

Grant me the confidence to do the work you require of me
And strength to bear the burdens life asks of me.

I swear to guard the Soul of Nature,
To work with Nature,
To honor Nature,
And all who compose nature's multitude.

These things I promise, and this I ask of you,
On this day, in this place.
As a green witch, I so swear.

ETHICS OF OUR PATH

In any path related to the expression of spirituality, the concept of ethics is important. Interestingly enough, there are no ethical or moral rules associated with the green witch path other than those that the practitioner already possesses. Why are there no ethical rules set out in green witchcraft practice?

Individuality

The practice is so very personal that to create an overarching ethical system would exclude some practitioners or force them to change who they are.

Green witchcraft isn't about forcing an individual to change; it's about an individual choosing to harmonize her own life with the energy of nature.

Connectedness

The green witch is so in tune with her surroundings that a set of ethical strictures is unnecessary. Knowing yourself to be a part of a greater whole makes it difficult to act against that whole.

Working with the earth means that to act against the greater whole would be counterproductive, and that includes acting against a member of the earth's extended energy, such as other people, animals, and plants.

It is difficult to act unethically when you understand how everyone and everything is affected by the negative actions.

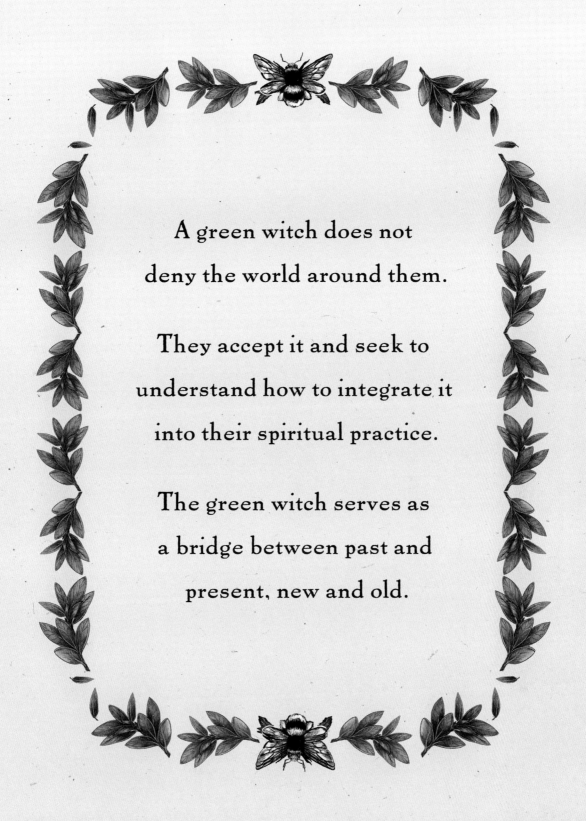

A green witch does not
deny the world around them.

They accept it and seek to
understand how to integrate it
into their spiritual practice.

The green witch serves as
a bridge between past and
present, new and old.

Meditation

We grow as people, shaped and affected by our experiences. It only makes sense to reassess and rededicate every once in a while. Our paths change, altered by our steps; a new location (physical, geographic, or spiritual) can call for a new statement of intention. Give yourself the gift of rededication. This can be done annually, or anytime you feel it necessary.

REDEDICATION TO THE PATH

Spirits of Nature,
You who have guided my feet and my heart,
I thank you for your presence in my life.
Your lessons, revelations, and inspiration have brought me to this point.
In this place, at this time, on this path,
I pause to affirm my dedication to walking the path of the green witch.
I promise to continue to honor the needs of the natural world,
To seek new lessons and deepen my experience.
May I continue to be blessed,
And to serve you with love and honor.

The History of Green Witchcraft

The practices of the modern green witch have arisen from folk healers and practitioners of folk magic. The modern green witch finds their foremothers and forefathers in village herbalists, midwives, healers, wisepeople, and cunning folk who performed particular services for their communities.

The duties of these spiritual ancestors of the green witch usually included midwifery and preparation of the dead for burial, as well as the use of various plants to heal mind and body. These people possessed knowledge of both life and death. They knew what kinds of which flora could create both states of existence. These earlier green witches, while often respected, could be feared or mistrusted because of the knowledge they held. They were often marginalized by their communities and lived alone or away from the social center of the community.

Even today, society is often uncomfortable with those who possess knowledge not held by the common man.

SIMILAR PATHS

There are other modern paths that resemble the path of the green witch.
Kitchen witches and hedge witches observe similar practices, and, indeed,
sometimes people use these terms interchangeably with green witchcraft.
All three paths have three basic things in common: they are based in folk magic,
they do not require a spiritual element, and walkers on all three paths tend to
be solitary practitioners.

Kitchen Witches

Family oriented and focus on magic
performed in the heart of the
modern home: the kitchen.

Bases their magical practice in their
everyday household activities, and
cooking, cleaning, baking, and so
forth all become the foundation for
their magical acts.

Sweeping the floor free of dust and
dirt may inspire a simultaneous
cleansing of negative energy, for
example.

Hedge Witches

Live close to nature, often away
from urban areas. It's a term used
more in the UK than in the US.

When you think of the
classic wiseperson on the edge
of town who was visited for love
charms and healing potions, you
have a pretty decent idea of what a
hedge witch is.

The modern hedge witch
is usually a solo practitioner of a
neopagan path who uses spellcraft
as a basis for their work.

Green witchcraft is
an ongoing celebration of life.

Green witchcraft is a dialogue with nature, a practice that enriches both the green witch and the earth itself.

The exchange of energy produces manifold benefits that may be stated in simple terms: through this dialogue, we heal the earth and the earth heals us.

We seek harmony through our actions.

We look to balance energies that are askew.

LEARN to IDENTIFY with the EARTH

The main identifying trait of green practice is a close identification with the earth. The green witch is not necessarily a member of an alternative spiritual path. The main difference between the green path and the neopagan religions is that godforms are not an essential part of a green witch's practice. While the green witch is content to look to mythology and ancient religions in order to deepen personal understanding of how earth energy has been perceived throughout the ages, they do not necessarily worship the gods and goddesses that are expressions and representations of earth patterns and energy.

Whereas alternative religions promote the idea that humanity is a steward or custodian of the planet, the green witch understands that they are the manifestation of the earth itself, not merely a caretaker. That close sense of identification allows them to work in partnership with the earth's energies.

" Think of the love and respect you
have for the earth.

Extend that regard to all
the creatures that make up the
natural world.

Humans, animals, plants,
trees—they are all part of nature.

Naturally, you treat them with
the same respect with which
you treat the earth herself. "

The path of the green witch is not by definition a religious one. It is a spiritual path, yes, but spirituality does not necessarily equate to religion. A green witch can participate in any religion and honor the divine in their own way, provided that they still honor nature as sacred and blessed.

The green witch sees the divine in all of nature, and each green witch interprets that divinity a little bit differently.

Like other earth-honoring paths, the roots of green witchcraft can be found in the agricultural calendar, seasonal shifts, weather patterns, and folk magic performed for health or fertility. Much of the modern neopagan practice comes from basic green witchcraft practice. Note that the word "roots" is key here: when something is rooted, it springs from a source, but it is still strong and anchored. To deny roots is to deny both foundation and strength. We may see only the trunk and the branches of a tree, but the root system ranges deep and wide.

Gratitude for Growth and Experience

Whether this is your introduction to green witchcraft, or a moment of gratitude on an established path, taking the time to mark your feelings about being here allows you to acknowledge your previous experience as well as your thankfulness to have found the path now before you. Here is an offering in recognition of your journey to your present position.

I call to the spirits of the elements, the sun, and the moon,
To acknowledge the experiences that brought me to the green witch path.

I have grown and deepened my knowledge,
Made the best choices from among those available to me,
And am grateful to find myself here.

My past has shaped me.
My present inspires me.
I will define my future, as I walk the path of the green witch.

Not all pasts were positive. You can acknowledge that too. If pain, exclusion, or cruelty were what helped you decide to find a different path to follow, you can acknowledge that, without being grateful for the negative experiences you endured. You can frame the gratitude as relief, as healing, or whatever you are called to see them as. You can celebrate the new path.

Natural Magic

Using the word "witch" invariably brings us to the word "magic." This is a word that can cause confusion. Magic is not illusion, nor is it the artificial manipulation of unnatural forces. In fact, magic is perfectly natural: it is the use of natural energy with conscious intent and awareness to help attain a better understanding of the world around you and to harmonize yourself with the world's energies.

Most green witches find the use of the word "magic" to be irrelevant. Magic implies something out of the ordinary. But to a green witch the mundane is magical. When we sense, respond to, and gently nudge the flows of natural energy around us, nothing could be more natural. We're performing natural magic. Nature itself is magical. The everyday is sacred to the green witch.

Marian Green, the author of *Wild Witchcraft*, believes that magic and nature are intertwined. In Green's view, magic is learning to harmonize yourself with the forces of nature and understanding how they flow through your life. This is, of course, the lifework of the green witch in a nutshell.

"Magic is the art of learning to recognize these elements of change: the natural patterns of flow and ebb, the times of progress, of standing still and of retreating… Magic teaches us to determine which way the tides of Nature are flowing, to see on which level they run and what they can offer each of us at this moment."

—Marian Green, author of *Wild Witchcraft*

Is brewing a cup of rosemary tea for a headache a spell?
Or is it natural medicine?

To the green witch, it doesn't really matter. What does matter is
the conscious use of the natural flow energies of the rosemary to
help heal a temporary imbalance.

It is the connection to the natural world and the knowing that
we are all a part of that world that allows us to function as a link
between the world of people and the world of green. In short,
by opening yourself to the energy of nature, and by accepting
that you are a part of that grand symphony of
energy and power, you allow yourself to
partake of that energy to rebalance
your life. Then you can work to
rebalance the energies of other
situations.

In other witchcraft practices, there are methods by which energy is raised, aimed at a target or goal, and released.

The green witch uses energy in a slower, more subtle way. Seeking to be a part of the ebb and flow of the energy around them, they thus do not deliberately collect energy to shape and release.

The green witch works from the inside out and moves with the natural flow of the energies instead of seeking to manipulate them.

Spellcraft is seen as a perfectly natural occurrence along the green path.

The magic is life itself.

Using the word "magic" can lead you to view
your green witch work as something set apart.
In this book, there are no rules for creating
a magic circle in which you must work, no
compulsory calling on deities, no sequences of
formal ritual that must be enacted precisely
as written. The practice of the green witch
is a fluid, natural, personal practice, one
that informs every moment of every day.
It is important to recognize each moment as
"magical" and full of potential. Everything is
magical, in the sense that it is wondrous and
unique—every breath, every step, every stir of
your soup.

Every act is an act of magic.

As a green witch, you carry a sacred responsibility not only to watch over the harmony of your environment, but also to remember that, as author Poppy Palin says in *Craft of the Wild Witch*:

> Every positive gesture has the potential to become a spell.

However, there is a danger in the practice of green witchcraft that familiarity may breed contempt. Recognizing each moment as magical and full of potential, the green witch may end up desensitizing themself to the point where no moment is special. Beware of falling into this rut. Allow yourself to marvel frequently at the joy and power of nature as the seasons cycle through the year, at the beautiful and frightful aspects of sunsets and storms. Every moment is magical because it holds potential, but also because it is merely a moment. The mundane is sacred to the green witch because it is mundane. The word "mundane" itself is derived from the Latin *mundus*, meaning "of the material world," and it is the energy created by the material world that sources the green witch's power.

Meditation

If the idea of a daily prayer appeals to you, this is a lovely way to begin or end your day. Try praying, aloud or in your heart, in a space that is sacred to you, one that is either formally blessed and consecrated or simply blessed by use in daily life.

The practice of the green witch doesn't have a lot of bells and whistles, fancy tools, or complicated rituals. Perhaps more than any other path of witchcraft, the path of the green witch rests on your philosophy of living and how you interact with the world around you. For this reason, your prayers, the rituals you perform, and your sacred space must be personally meaningful. Creating a personal practice that reflects who you are and your desire to create harmony in the world around you is the key to living a fulfilling life as a green witch.

PRAYER OF THE GREEN WITCH

Lord and Lady,
Spirits of Nature,
Elements around me,
Bless me as I move through the world today.

May I bring joy and tranquility to every life I touch.
May my actions bring only harmony to the world.
May I heal pain and soothe anger,
May I create joy and balance as I walk my path.

Support me and guide me, spirits of Nature,
This day and all days ahead of me.
This I ask of you, as a green witch,
And thank you for your many blessings.

CHAPTER 2

EMBRACE
Your Own
POWER

reen witchcraft emphasizes practicality and everyday activity. There are no special words, no unique prayers, no uniforms, no holy texts, no obligatory tools, and no specific holidays... unless you create them for yourself. While the green path is very much the art of daily practice, it isn't set apart as sacred. It recognizes the sacred in everyday life.

That being said, the green witch path can be said to focus on certain issues and energies experienced in the secular life. The green witch's practice revolves around working toward establishing and maintaining harmony within oneself, within one's community, and with nature.

FOCUS on YOUR CORE ENERGIES

There are seven basic areas
or energies on which the green
witch's practice focuses:

Harmony:
within the self;
between humanity and
nature; within a community
or family

Abundance:
personal;
familial;
community;
nation; nature

Love:
for the self;
for other individuals;
for humanity

Peace:
within oneself;
within a community
or family; between
nations

Protection:
personal;
familial; community;
nature

Health:
of the body, mind,
and spirit; of the
environment

Happiness:
in oneself;
in others;
in the natural
world

We will return again and again to these seven categories as we explore the practice of the green witch. You'll also see these focal areas mentioned with recipes and rituals to help you understand the purposes for which they may be used. Let's look at them one by one. Each one is accompanied by a flower that represents it.

HARMONY

Harmony is the main goal of the green witch's practice. Harmony can be seen as the energy that helps all the other energies flow and is capable of being applied to any of the other six areas of focus to help them along.

Gardenia

> To maintain harmony, you must balance the six other areas of your life, and when everything is in harmony, these other six areas will flow smoothly and in balance.

When your personal energy is balanced and all the various parts of yourself are in tune, you are in harmony with yourself. That's harder to achieve than it sounds. We all possess traits that we dislike and wish we didn't have. It's important, however, to acknowledge those bits of your personality and spirit, for if you deny them then you are attempting to reject a part of yourself, and you thus deny part of your own energy. In doing so, you deny part of your connection to nature. Harmony between humankind and nature is important and fostering that balance between humanity and the natural world is part of the green witch's work.

HEALTH

Health affects your physical well-being, certainly, but it also affects your emotional, mental, and spiritual well-being. Listening to and working with your own body's energy will help you maintain a balanced and healthy mind and spirit. All of these energies are interdependent and deserve to be taken into account when one or another goes out of equilibrium.

Sunflower

LOVE

Most people spend a lot of energy on love: attempting to find it, keep it, or strengthen it. But there's more to love than the romantic kind. Healthy love of the self is crucial to a well-balanced personal energy and to healthy self-esteem. Love of family and close friends who form your chosen family is important, for it is the love of such companions that supports you in your everyday efforts. Loving others is an example of honoring and respecting nature and all nature's creatures: it is an act of honoring their very existence and their place within nature's energy.

Rose

HAPPINESS

There are many different kinds of happiness. Your own joy, for example, is one goal, but you can also work for the happiness of others and of the natural world. Remember that happiness is very much a personal thing, and that no one act or item will make everyone happy. Happiness also encompasses the ability to rejoice and celebrate the self, and each person celebrates the self in a unique fashion.

Lilac

PEACE

Violet

Peace can mean a variety of different things depending on your need: serenity, relaxation, an absence of aggression, and tranquility, for example. Like happiness, peace is a highly individual concept. The green witch works for tranquility and peace, for in a peaceful environment energies that would otherwise be directed toward defense can instead be directed toward more productive and positive actions.

ABUNDANCE

Tulip

Abundance is an area of focus that encompasses such energies as prosperity and fertility. When you have an abundance of something, you no longer worry about it. You feel secure enough to focus on areas of your life that require your attention in order to bring them into balance. As with the other areas of focus, the green witch may look to personal, familial, and community abundance, as well as to ensuring the fertility and abundance of the natural world.

PROTECTION

Geranium

Protection involves safeguarding something precious. It can be protecting your physical body or the bodies of others, your possessions, your emotional well-being, the soul or spirit of an individual, the well-being of a family or community, or the natural world, either locally or globally. When we are protected, we feel safe and free to pursue other avenues of self-expression and development.

Acknowledging Responsibility As a Green Witch

Acknowledging your own power can be difficult. It may feel presumptuous or arrogant. However, it's an important step in the process of confirming your partnership with the energy of the natural world. Affirming your participation in the give-and-take flow and dialogue with nature is to acknowledge your responsibility as part of the process. You are an active participant, not a passive object buffeted about. You are aware, and that awareness comes with responsibility. This prayer can be said to confirm your commitment whenever you feel moved to do it.

I acknowledge my responsibility as a participant
In the cycle of energy around me.

I acknowledge my responsibility as a green witch to monitor the land,
The plants and trees, and the creatures who live among them all.
I acknowledge those who came before me in this place,
Their wisdom and their care,
And the energies of the native species that make this place their home.

I vow to uphold these responsibilities to the best of my ability,
Seeking health, safety, and peace for all.

Tools of Use

Because green witchcraft isn't an organized path, there are no required tools or equipment you must have in order to follow it. There are, however, important items almost every green witch uses in her practice.

Your Hands

A green witch's hands are their most valuable tools. With our hands, we touch and take in information. With our hands, we dispense caring. Our sense of touch is a keen one. You use your hands to tend and harvest your herbs and plants, prepare them for storage, and blend them together. Your hands can become a physical extension of your thoughts and your will.

Herbs and Plants

With so much emphasis on working with natural energies, it is not surprising that herbs and plants immediately come to mind when one thinks about a green witch and the things they use or interact with. Chapter 5 looks at common trees, flowers, and plants used by the green witch.

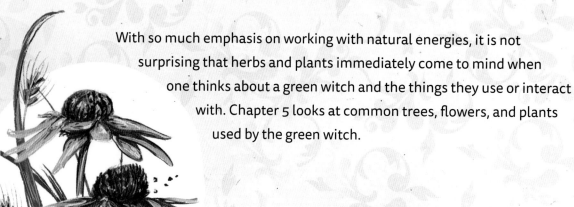

MORTAR AND PESTLE

A mortar and pestle is invaluable for crushing dried herbs, seeds, or resins and for blending materials for a variety of projects. Stone is the easiest material to keep clean and has the weight and strength required to crush things like resins. The standard size mortar is approximately 5 inches high by about 5 inches wide, with a slightly tapered pestle of about 4 inches by 1 inch. You really shouldn't use anything smaller.

POWER BAGS

As a green witch, you will develop a personal connection to little objects such as stones, acorns, pinecones, or fetishes, and you may wish to carry them with you. Sew up or buy a small bag to hold them and slip it into your purse or backpack when you travel. By doing this, you carry the natural energy of those objects along with you so that they influence your own energy.

CUP

A simple cup (ceramic is ideal) is a useful item for the green witch. Water is one of the four physical (and metaphysical) elements, and a cup reserved exclusively to hold water in this way honors the element of water. In addition, the cup is useful to drink from in a ritual setting. A familiar tool such as a cup can lend a certain energy to your work if it is reserved only for your green witch use.

44

JOURNAL

Recording your journey is of great importance because this record forms the main body of lore to which you will refer again and again in your work. Your journal is not meant to be perfect. It's meant to be a real-life snapshot of your thoughts and evolving knowledge. It will contain some magical information, yes, because the green witch understands that magic is simply another method of touching the energy of the earth; but mainly it will contain:

Rituals	Explorations
Recipes	Field Notes
Projects	Sketches
Experiments	Research
Observations	Maps

When you ramble through a field or forest or go for walks through your neighborhood, make sure you have your green witch notebook with you. If carrying your main journal is difficult because of its size, you may wish to have a smaller field book in which to make notes while you are out. Transfer information you have picked up on your treks into your main journal when you get home again. Your green witch journal will prove important and helpful to you in months and years to come.

COTTON OR GAUZE

A roll of natural cotton about 6–8 inches wide and a couple of feet long is a useful item to carry with you when you walk in forest or meadow. It may be used to roll herbs in, instead of putting them in a bag, and can help preserve more fragile cuttings. It's also good for first aid use, should you cut yourself, scratch yourself, or incur other minor damage along the way.

BOWLS

Bowls in which to mix and hold ingredients are essential to your work. An assortment of small ceramic ramekins will do for many projects. Do not use plastic bowls as they absorb oils and scents. Glass or glazed ceramic bowls are the best choice.

JARS AND CANISTERS

To store your herbs, incenses, and other ingredients, glass or ceramic jars or canisters are ideal. Like your bowls, these can range in size. Colored glass or an opaque material will help protect your dried herbs from fading and losing their beneficial oils.

KNIFE OR SCISSORS

An essential green witch tool is the sharp knife used to harvest herbs and other plants. This knife must be kept extremely clean and must always be sharp, for a dull blade is dangerous to both the one who uses it and that which is being cut. If you are uncomfortable using a straight knife to cut stems and leaves, you may prefer a pair of good sharp shears or scissors instead.

STAFF

A staff or walking stick not only helps you as you ramble through the natural world, but it also serves as a symbolic "world tree," which connects the material and spiritual realms. The world tree is like the world's spine, serving as a support and a connection between the otherworlds and the world of humankind.

The tree is a remarkable symbol. We perceive trees as being strong and offering us shelter or support, and yet we also see them as being flexible, for some trees bend in the wind. The roots of a tree can reach deep into the earth for stability and for nourishment. Its branches reach high into the sky so that the leaves of the tree may absorb as much sunlight as possible and further nourish the tree. A staff or walking stick symbolizes all this in miniature. It is a symbol of the tree, carries a tree's energy, and reminds the green witch of the connection to both earth and sky.

Your Home is a Sacred Space

Most people on the green witch path have a strong connection to their surroundings. They instinctively seek to create an environment that supports harmony, communication, and a natural flow of energy.

In the past, the hearth served as the heart of the home. It was where heat and light were created and food was prepared. Hearth magic, or hearthcraft, revolves around safety, nurturing, and protection. Most paths have a hearth and home aspect to them, but for the green witch, so much of her spiritual practice is focused on simple home-based folk practices that hearth magic figures prominently in her green practice.

Your home itself—the space in which you live—can be easily overlooked as a tool in your developing spirituality. Your home is a place of strength for you, and a place to which you should be able to return in safety to renew your energy.

TIPS for YOUR HOME

How do you make your home a sacred space? Ultimately, it depends on you and the type of energy that supports your daily life.

If your home is disorganized and has jarring energy, you lack that base of strength from which you must operate. Here are actions to make your home the best place for a green witch to live. These tips will help keep positive energy flowing through your home.

ᴥ Reduction ᴥ

If you aren't using it, throw it out. Otherwise, it's just occupying space and blocking energy. Sell it, pass it along to a friend, take it to a secondhand shop, or find another use for it somewhere else.

ᴥ Cleanliness ᴥ

Energy can seem dusty and muddy, the same way your physical home gets dirty. It's also an unfortunate fact that energy turns stale and can go bad in an environment that isn't physically clean. Make sure everything has a place and keep it there. Keep surfaces free of dust and clutter as best you can.

❧ Décor ❧

Look at your home with fresh and critical eyes. Do the colors reflect who you are? What does the furniture say about you? Walk through each room. Are there places you have to struggle to get to? If you don't want to go there because it's too difficult, then chances are good that the energy flow through that area gets dammed up or otherwise slowed down. Think about rearranging the positions of furniture, pictures, and knickknacks.

❧ Purpose ❧

When you decide what the theme or purpose of each room truly is, you can focus on removing the elements that disrupt the energy. Try to keep each room clearly set apart for its designated purpose, and you'll find that the energy is a lot clearer. If a room serves a double purpose, keep things in their proper places.

❧ Iconography ❧

Your paintings and photographs have a deep psychological effect on you. Take a look at the colors that dominate them and the people in them. How do they make you feel? Are they appropriate for the space they're in?

❧ Purification ❧

The spiritual equivalent of physical cleaning, purification is an excellent way to maintain good energy in your home. It's also a good way to get rid of the bad feelings left over from an argument. You can find instructions on how to purify later in this chapter.

ROOM BY ROOM

Sometimes we look around our homes and wonder how on earth we can make them a haven of tranquility and joy. Starting off with a good spring cleaning (even if it's fall!) is always a good idea. If the idea of addressing your whole house at once is overwhelming, do it room by room. To begin, you can choose one room to serve as a spiritual sanctuary and refuge for yourself. Or, you can start from the heart of your home and work outward.

Your Sanctuary

Your sanctuary doesn't have to be a space solely devoted to you and your path; in fact, most of us share space with our family or other people and make do with carving out a corner where we can. You just need a place where you can sit and close your eyes, draw that tranquility into your personal space, and find balance.

Heart of Your Home

The heart of your home can be easier to identify than your sanctuary. Do people tend to end up in your kitchen? Does your family congregate in one room? Where people gather is likely the true heart of your home. It's not necessarily a tranquil space and usually sees a lot of comings and goings.

Physical Cleaning, Spiritual Purification

When you clean, you can further visualize the energy you are calling into the space. Visualizing while you clean also helps take away the boredom and resentment we associate with removing the dust and dirt that will just build up again anyway. Think of it as green witch maintenance of your personal space.

The second dimension to keeping your space clean and bright is purification. It's important to clean the energy of your living space because the energy of an environment affects the energy of the people functioning within it.

Empower Your Cleaning Tools

The simplest way to enhance your housecleaning products is to empower them. This means filling them with extra energy associated with a particular goal. Here's how to do it:

1. First hold the container of cleaning product in your hands, or hold your hands over it, and close your eyes.
2. Take three or four deep breaths to calm and balance yourself.
3. Think of the energy with which you wish to empower the product to help you attain your goal. For example, you could focus on happiness. Try to remember how you feel when you're happy.
4. Now try to pour that feeling into the cleaning product. Visualize the feeling welling up from your heart and flowing down your arms and out through your hands; see the product absorbing that energy.
5. Now when you clean with it, you'll be using the physical product to clean, but while cleaning you will also be filling the area with the energy with which the product was empowered. You can empower your cleaning supplies with more than one energy as long as those energies support one another and aren't at cross-purposes. For the best results, choose earth-friendly, organic, or fair trade cleaning products that carry no toxic ingredients.

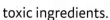

If you've ever walked into a room and felt odd for no obvious reason, then you've been affected by the energy present in that space. While it's true that the physical state of cleanliness affects the energy of a room, you have to clean the existing energy of a room as well. Otherwise, the negative energy will pile up, just as dust collects on a bookshelf.

Purification can be done in several ways. A classic method is to sweep the negative energy away with a broom. The witch's broom is often seen only as a symbol, but it can also be used as a regular tool. It can, in fact, be a remarkably useful item, and it's very easy to use.

Broom Purification

This basic purification with a broom can be done almost anytime and anywhere. Do not use a plastic or nylon-bristled broom. Find one with real straw bristles. (For a personal touch, you can make one yourself following the directions in Chapter 7.) You can keep the broom you use for purification for that purpose alone, or use your regular housecleaning broom to purify.

YOU WILL NEED

A broom

STEPS TO TAKE

1. Stand in the middle of the room you intend to purify. Hold the broom in your hands. Take three deep, slow breaths to calm yourself.
2. Begin to make a sweeping motion, sweeping the broom from your right to your left. Don't touch the floor with the broom, but swing the broom an inch or so above it. It's energy you're sweeping, not the floor itself.
3. Turning to your left, slowly turn in place. This is a counterclockwise direction, which is traditionally associated with breaking up and banishing negative energy. Walk in a counterclockwise spiral around the room, sweeping just above the floor as you go. As you walk and sweep, visualize the energy of the room being stirred up by the motion of your broom, and any heavy spots being broken up and restored to the regular flow. See the energy being transformed from murky to bright and sparkling.
4. Sweep the entire room, gradually widening your counterclockwise spiral until you end at the door. If you wish, you may end the purification with a statement, such as: *Bright and strong flows the energy through my home. This room is purified.*

Room Purification Incense

A wonderful way to purify a room is with this gentle incense that releases energy associated with clearing negativity. Burn a pinch of it on a self-lighting charcoal briquette (*not* barbecue charcoal; see Chapter 7) in a heatproof censer or dish. This recipe will make about 1 tablespoon of incense.

YOU WILL NEED

1 teaspoon frankincense resin

1 teaspoon copal resin

Mortar and pestle (optional)

1 teaspoon dried powdered lemon zest

3 pinches dried lavender

Small glass jar with tight-fitting lid

STEPS TO TAKE

1. If necessary, gently grind the resins with a mortar and pestle until the pieces are in small granules. Be careful not to overgrind them, or they will become sticky.

2. Add all the ingredients to the jar, cap it, and shake until the ingredients are well blended.

3. Hold the jar and visualize a sparkling light forming around it. This sparkling light is purifying energy to empower the incense. Visualize the sparkling light being absorbed into the blend of resins and herbs.

4. Label and date the jar. To use the incense, light a charcoal briquette and place it within the censer as instructed in Chapter 7. Take a pinch of the purification incense and sprinkle it on top of the charcoal. Place in the middle of the room and allow the purifying energy to fill the room.

MAKE a SACRED OUTDOOR SPACE

If you are fortunate enough to be a green witch with a bit of green space behind or in front of your home, there are a few things you can do with this space to make it vibrant and more sacred.

If you own or rent land, then you may consider creating a small outdoor sacred space in which you can relax, rebalance, and reconnect with the natural world. A small corner, a garden bench, or even a single stone set into a small flower bed can serve as your sacred space. Choose anything that has meaning to you.

Sacred space can also be a small area that only you recognize as being dedicated to your spirituality. You can choose a set of plants that symbolize your practice and plant them together. You can place a stone among the plants, or a small all-weather statue, or a trellis upon which you can hang a tiny set of wind chimes. Your corner of outdoor sacred space should offer you a place to sit or stand to pause and clear your mind, to touch Spirit, and to rebalance yourself.

Options for achieving reconnection and rebalancing are also available for the modern green witch in an urban setting:

1.

Visit your city parks or public gardens to find a place that feels comfortable and calm to you. Your city may even have a community garden that you can join.

2.

Set up a container garden on your balcony. You can grow flowers, vegetables, and herbs.

3.

Bring nature indoors. Carefully selected houseplants can also furnish you with a connection to a sacred space with the feeling of outdoors.

> **The most powerful magic you can create comes from you and your connection to your local energies.**

CHAPTER 3

ATTUNE YOURSELF *to* NATURE

reen witchcraft is always about the now, about the current state of your environment. Being aware of your environment means knowing the energies moving through it, the energies it produces, its health and rate of vibration. It also means being aware of how your own energy and mental or emotional state fit into your surroundings. You may think you know your environment, but you might be surprised when you stop to create a new relationship with it. One of the basic foundations of living the green witch path is forging a connection with nature and natural forces. It is imperative that you forge that connection with what is actually there, and not what you assume to be there.

GET to KNOW YOUR CORNER of the UNIVERSE

If you live in an urban setting, then that city's energy is the energy to which you must open yourself in order to be in tune with your neighborhood and your environment. It is crucial to interact with your natural environment as it actually is, not the nature you imagine or idealize. The environment you knew yesterday or last month is no longer the environment that surrounds you: energy is in a state of constant change. Thus, the green witch must also be aware, and always adjusting their knowledge.

You may think you know your neighborhood, but it's useful to take the time to see it in a new way. Use all your senses to explore where you live. Ask yourself the following questions:

What wild plants are common to your neighborhood? Can you name at least ten local plants?

How do the seasons change where you live? What changes can you see and feel?

What trees are most commonly found? Which are indigenous? Which were deliberately introduced? When and by whom?

Is the water that's channeled to your tap hard or soft?

What type of soil does your neighborhood have? Is it chalky, clayey, sandy, or other? Is it alkaline or acidic?

What wildlife is native to your area?

Taking the time to learn more about your neighborhood will give you a good solid base from which to learn more about how your natural environment functions. Walking around with enhanced awareness can teach you more than you thought you knew.

Interaction Exercises

When observation is done with intent, you will discover more about your neighborhood. For this exercise, first choose a stone or a plant that you're familiar with. Allow yourself to experience it again as if for the first time. Answer the following questions.

Write your answers in your green witch journal. This exercise is designed to help you observe as much as you can and make the most of each experience as you gather information.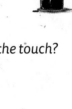

What does this stone or plant feel like to the touch?
How does it smell?
What does it look like?
What sounds does it make?
How does it taste?

Caution! Try to catch the taste on the air. Never place an unidentified plant or object in your mouth.

Once you've done this exercise with a few plants or stones you're already familiar with, try one you've not experienced before. Notes on these exercises will serve as the basis of your green witch lore and become the heart of your personal practice.

"The natural world sings. Its rhythms thrum throughout our lives, entwined with our daily steps."

EXPERIENCE the ENERGY AROUND YOU

Although the green witch uses herbs for their medicinal qualities, the magical qualities of the natural world are also very much our friends. The medicinal benefits often parallel the magical uses. This is because, in addition to a certain chemical makeup that determines its effect when applied to the physical body, an herb also possesses a unique energy that affects the emotions and spirit of a person. Your observations of the energy of the plant are valid because they're yours. Everyone interacts differently with the energy of a plant. If lavender energizes you, then that is one of lavender's energy benefits in your practice, even though many books will tell you that lavender projects feelings of peace and tranquility. Acquiring firsthand knowledge is important for a green witch, as it shapes and refines your practice, personalizing it in a way that makes it truly unique.

Sensing Energy

Perform this exercise with a plant with which you are familiar, then try it with something you've never seen or handled before. Trust your observations.

YOU WILL NEED

For this exercise, you'll need the plant,
plus your green witch journal and a pen or pencil.

STEPS TO TAKE

1. Take the plant in your hand. If it is a dried or harvested herb, hold a pinch in your palm or hold your hand over it, palm down. If it is a living plant that you have correctly identified as safe to touch, gently touch it with your fingers. If you cannot identify it, hold your hand above or to the side of the plant with your palm toward it.

2. Close your eyes and imagine your palm glowing. Focus on the sensation of your palm. It may tingle or grow warm or cool. That means you're focusing on the energy your palm is creating naturally.

3. Visualize the plant glowing.

4. Visualize the glow of energy collected in your palm gently stretching out to touch the glowing energy of the plant. As the two energies meet, ask yourself what you sense.

Do you feel a specific emotion?
Do ideas drift into your head? Thoughts?
Do you sense vague hunches?

Pay attention. This is a method for collecting observations about the plant by sensing its energy with your own energy.

5. When you feel you have observed enough, send the plant a feeling of gratitude for its cooperation, then visualize your energy disengaging from that of the plant and drawing back into your palm.

6. Open your eyes and shake your hand firmly, as if you're shaking water off of it. This will help you get rid of any excess energy hanging on.

7. Write your observations in your green witch journal.

What was the experience like?
What sort of observations did you make?
Did the plant feel energetic, calming, nurturing?

Write down everything that comes to you and don't worry about whether it makes sense or not.

GROUND YOURSELF

When you work with energy, it is important to ground yourself. Grounding means connecting your personal energy to that of the earth and allowing a rebalancing of your energy to occur. If you are nervous or excited, you may be running too much energy through your body. The earth is a good place to shunt that extra energy. If you are lethargic or dizzy, you may be suffering from a lack of energy, and the earth has plenty to share with you. Once you are grounded, you can absorb the energy of the earth to replenish your low energy levels.

Grounding

Grounding is good to do when you get up in the morning, last thing at night, before you do any energy work, or whenever you feel a little out of sync with the world around you. To ground yourself, follow these steps:

1. Take three deep, slow breaths.
2. Next take a moment to feel your own energy flowing through your body. Focus on a point in the center of your chest and visualize a small green glowing light there. This is your energy center.
3. Now visualize a tendril of green energy growing from that energy center down toward the earth. Let it reach down past your feet. Visualize it growing into the earth itself, spreading into roots and twisting through the soil. Take a moment to feel how solid and stable your root is in the earth.
4. Now that you have formed a connection with the earth, you can either allow your excess energy to flow down to mingle with that of the earth or draw some of the earth's energy up to replace the energy you are missing.

WORK with the FOUR NATURAL ELEMENTS

The four physical elements form the building blocks of a green witch's understanding of the world around them. They represent the raw material of nature. The flow and interaction between the four basic elemental energies form the basis of change, transformation, growth, evolution, and development in our environment and in our lives. Each element has a specific energy. Traditionally, they have the associations described here.

Fire

Passion
Creativity
Projective
Active

Air

Communication
Intellect
Projective
Active

Earth

Grounding
Abundance
Receptive
Passive

Water

Emotion
Sensitivity
Receptive
Passive

Although the four elements are always present, you can choose to recognize them in your practice by formally inviting one or more of the elements to aid you in your green witch work.

This formal invitation is often called invoking the element.

Invoking an element is a conscious act that draws that element's energy to you in your environment. Invoking an element can be done if you want that element's particular aid or energy to blend with the work you are doing. For example, if you are creating a garden sachet for fertility in your vegetable garden, then you may invoke the element of earth to be present while you construct the sachet and weave the elemental energy into the energy of the sachet to help support and reinforce it. Many green witches like to work with a symbol of each element nearby, which honors the elements and creates a balanced atmosphere in which to work. Those symbols can be as simple as:

Fire	Air	Earth	Water

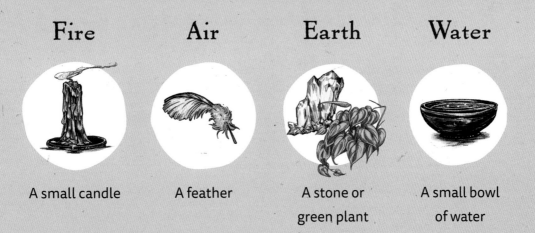

| A small candle | A feather | A stone or green plant | A small bowl of water |

Sensing the Four Elements Exercise

This exercise helps you build a personal relationship with each element. To keep yourself attuned to the basic energies produced by the elements, perform this exercise at least once a year. Before you begin, review the previous energy-sensing exercise.

YOU WILL NEED

Your green witch journal and a pen

Small dish of earth*

Hand fan or a small piece of card stock

Votive candle in a candleholder

Matches or a lighter

Small dish of water

Small towel

STEPS TO TAKE

1. Open your journal and prepare to write down your observations. For example, how did the exercise make you feel? What did the energy make you think of?

2. Begin by sitting quietly at a table or on the floor with the supplies set out in front of you. Take three deep breaths. As you exhale, visualize any tension leaving your body.

3. Visualize your fingertips glowing with your personal energy. Visualize the sample of earth glowing with the energy of earth. Gently reach out and rest your fingertips on the soil (or salt or stone or crystal). Close your eyes. Allow your personal energy to contact the soil's energy. While connected to the earth energy, observe how it makes you feel. When you are finished, withdraw your fingers and brush them off if necessary. Shake your hand to remove any excess energy or odd sensations. Open your journal and write down your observations about the energy of the element of earth.

4. Pick up the hand fan or card stock in one hand, and hold your other hand out, palm up. Visualize the palm of your hand glowing with your personal energy. Close your eyes and slowly begin to wave the fan or card, creating an air current directed at your other palm. As the air moves, see it glow with the energy of air. Allow the energy of the air current to meet the energy of your palm and observe the sensations you pick up. Vary the speed of the air current and observe whether that makes a difference to your observations. When you are finished, set aside the fan and shake your hand to remove any excess energy or odd sensations. Write down your observations about the energy of the element of air in your journal.

5. Light the votive candle. Visualize the energy of your palm glowing. Visualize the flame of the candle glowing with the energy of fire. Hold your hand beside the flame at a safe and comfortable distance, and reach out to the energy of fire with your own energy. Observe as much as you can about the energy of fire. When you are finished, snuff out the candle and shake any excess energy off your hand. Write down your observations about the energy of the element of fire in your journal.

6. Bring the dish of water toward you. Visualize your fingertips glowing with your personal energy, and see water glowing with the energy of the element of water. Slowly touch the surface of the water with your fingertips and allow your personal energy to engage with the water's energy. Observe as much as you can about the energy of water. When you are finished, withdraw your fingers and wipe them on the small towel, then shake them to remove any excess energy. Write down your observations about the energy of the element of water in your journal.

Note: Make sure it's rich earth; if all you have is dry potting soil, use a dish of salt or a stone or a crystal.

DISCOVER YOUR SENSES

While everyone interfaces differently with the world around them, we all acquire information via our five senses.

Vision

Most people are primarily visual. Here are some exercises to help you develop how you use your sense of sight:

★ Look at a color photo of an apple, then at a real apple. How are they different to your eyes? How are they the same?

★ Set an everyday object on a table in front of you and look at it carefully. Then hold it above your normal eye level and look up at it. Set it on the floor and look down at it. Move it to the left, then to the right. How does the position of the object change how you see it?

★ Sit in front of a window, and use it as a frame for what you see through it. Allow yourself to really see things in detail, things you usually just glance at and take in during a split second.

Sound

Sound is overwhelmingly present in our lives. Our world is very rarely truly silent. Hearing helps us fill in what our vision reveals to us. Here are exercises to help you deepen your sense of hearing:

★ Sit in a familiar place in your home and close your eyes. Listen deliberately and with awareness to the sounds of your home. What do you hear? How many different sounds do you hear? Where are they coming from? Can you identify them?

★ Sit in a public place like a mall or a restaurant and perform this exercise again. Do it with a friend by your side so that you can relax and not worry about what's going on around you. How are the sounds different? How is the way you listen in public different from how you listen at home?

★ Sit outdoors and perform the exercise. Do you find it more difficult to identify outdoor sounds? Where do they come from? Do you hear more or fewer sounds than you hear indoors?

Touch   The sense of touch can be broken down into specific kinds of senses: the perception of pain, the perception of temperature, the perception of pressure, the perception of balance and equilibrium, and the perception of body awareness or location. Try these exercises to explore your sense of touch. If possible, do them with your eyes closed so you are not using sight to influence your sense of touch:

★ Find a patch of sun. Move your hand into the sun and feel its warmth. Move it back into the shadows and feel the absence of heat.

★ Gather a feather, a small bowl of salt, an ice cube in a small bowl or glass, a piece of wood, and a satin ribbon and set them on a table in front of you. One by one, explore the touch of each item. Pick the item up; stroke it with your fingertips and with your palm. Hold it in your hands and feel its weight. How does it feel if you hold it still? How does it feel if you move your hand while holding it?

★ Set a bowl of warm water and a bowl of cold water on the table in front of you. Sink the fingers of one hand into the bowl of warm water, leave them there for a minute, then remove them and put them into the bowl of cold water. How does the temperature contrast feel? After leaving your fingers in the cold water for a minute, dip them back into the warm water. Does the warm water feel different now?

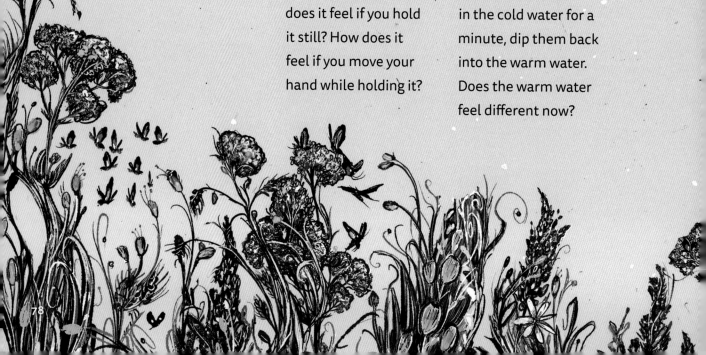

Taste

Our sense of taste is often drowned in excess. Fast food and canned meals have lowered our standards of taste to such an extent that if we taste fresh apple, the tangy flavor surprises our taste buds. We have become accustomed to dull, chemical-like tastes. To remind your taste buds of single flavors, do the following exercises:

★ On a table, set out a small bowl of salt, a small bowl of sugar, a small bowl of an herb such as rosemary, a segment of orange, a slice of lemon, a glass of water, and a slice of plain bread. Wash and dry your hands. Sit down and touch your finger to the salt, then touch your finger to your tongue. Allow the taste of the salt to spread across your tongue. How does it taste? Can you describe it without using the word "salty"? Cleanse your palate by taking a sip of water and a tiny bite of the bread. Repeat the action with the sugar, then cleanse your palate again. Continue along through the foods, taking the time to savor each flavor. Imagine you are tasting each food for the very first time.

★ Repeat the previous exercise when you take the first bite of your next meal. Taste each item on your plate slowly and carefully, and imagine you are tasting each one for the very first time.

Smell

We usually underestimate the power of our sense of smell. Smell is a delicate sense that picks up minute shifts in air currents, and it's often overwhelmed in the city by exhaust from cars, dirt and refuse, perfumes and overscented soaps, and the general effluvia of thousands of people living close together. Try these exercises to help deepen your understanding of your sense of smell:

★ Sit in a familiar place in your home and close your eyes. Breathe evenly. As you inhale, notice what scents you are smelling. What is the general overall scent of your home? Can you further identify the individual smells that constitute that overall scent?

★ Repeat this exercise in a public place, with a friend along to keep an eye on what's going on around you. When you close your eyes, how would you identify the location simply by its smell? Can you identify smaller, individual smells?

★ Repeat this exercise outdoors. Do you find it easier or more difficult to identify individual smells outside?

The Sixth Sense

Alongside the five basic physical senses, there is another method you use to gather information. This is the sense people call the sixth sense. Your sixth sense tells you that someone behind you is staring at you; even though you cannot use one of the five physical senses to confirm it, you can sense it. The green witch knows and understands that this sense cannot always be explained. We also acknowledge its existence and accept information acquired via the sixth sense. There are various explanations for how the sixth sense works. Some say that your personal energy field (sometimes referred to as the aura) picks up the energy fields of other things and information passes between them.

Living in an urban setting, people can become desensitized to the sights, smells, and sounds of their daily environment. A green witch should never allow themself to become desensitized, however, because they will miss minute shifts in energy, changes that may signal a problem of some kind. The old adage "familiarity breeds contempt" has application here as well.

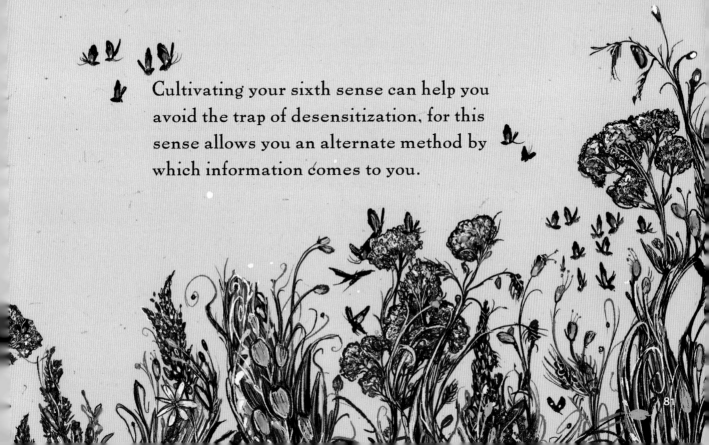

Cultivating your sixth sense can help you avoid the trap of desensitization, for this sense allows you an alternate method by which information comes to you.

Sharpen Your Intuition

A way to improve your relationship with nature and the web of energy that surrounds you is to work on developing your intuition.

Intuition is using information that your energy picks up from the energies around you. You may feel that you do that all the time. Isn't that what we do when we reach out to something to feel its energy? The answer is yes...and no. One is done with intention and awareness. Intuition is more akin to a subroutine that runs automatically without you paying close attention to it. It's always running, feeding you information that you don't consciously notice, but often use anyway. So, if it runs automatically without you paying attention to it, how would you exercise to improve it? The answer is to consciously practice working with it in short sessions, so that you can practice getting better at hearing the information it's passing to you. And, like any skill, the more you practice, the smoother it gets.

Exercise to Sharpen Your Intuition

As you set up, try not to observe too much of what's around you so as to not influence the exercise. To feel safe, you might ask a friend to accompany you to wherever you want to try this, so they can be watchful while you sit with your eyes closed.

1. Sit in your chosen place. Close your eyes. Say aloud or to yourself:

   I invoke my intuition.
   I open myself to information
   For my betterment, safety, and benefit.

2. Take a few moments to reach out and sense the energies around you. Ask yourself:

   How does this place make me feel?
   What do I sense ahead of me? To either side? Behind me?
   What emotions do I sense around me?
   What do I feel might happen in the next few minutes?

3. After each question, open your eyes and look around. Did you sense things close to what you can now physically see? Are there some things you missed? While observing the area afterward, does anything happen that resonates with what you intuited might happen?

Write your observations down in your green witch's journal when you're done. Take time to observe the area with all of your five physical senses to see if your intuition gave you information that supports the observations you made with the five traditional senses.

CHAPTER 4

MANIFEST THE POWER
of the
SEASONS

Awareness of the natural rhythm of the solstices and equinoxes and how they are reflected in your location form the axis of the green witch's practice. The solar year is made up of four distinct seasons, each with resonance for the green witch. These four seasons can provide the basis for personal practice and the creation of a unique tradition specific to you as an individual green witch.

The four seasons also allow you to formally recognize the flow of seasonal energy and honor it. Set aside some time on or around the first day of each season to meditate upon the changes in energy that you are feeling in your environment.

Seasonal Cycles and Energy

No matter where you live, your weather cycles form a recognizable pattern over a full calendar year. The vegetation grows and falls back in a pattern over the year. The animal population follows certain behavioral patterns. As the earth's angle and distance from the sun change, the seasonal cycle embodies the basic relationship between light and dark. The concept of darkness is necessary in the natural cycle: without darkness, there can be no fallow period during which the earth regains its strength, seeds will not germinate, animals will not bear their young in season.

When we observe the four seasons, we can categorize the climate shifts and environmental responses that occur over the calendar year. When we observe a certain event happening in the natural world, for example, we can say, "Ah, now it is spring." We all have personal associations with seasonal events that really bring home what time of year it is. These associations are part of our personal connection with the natural world around us. There is no right or wrong way to observe a solstice or an equinox. Every green witch creates their own tradition, their own expression of the seasons and how they change. That unique expression will reflect how the season affects their spirit, their heart, and their body.

In North America, there are four seasons that begin on specific days and at specific times.

Although the seasons are determined by the astronomical position of the sun and the earth, meteorologically the following approximate dates are used to mark the beginning of spring, summer, autumn, and winter:

Spring equinox ● March 21
Summer solstice ● June 21
Autumn equinox ● September 21
Winter solstice ● December 21

EAST

If a different date in these months makes more sense to you where you live and corresponds to how seasonal differences manifest in your environment, why not use them? The point of living as a green witch is to be in tune with your surroundings. Adhering to a date simply because it is a standard date does not always make sense when it comes to celebrating the changing seasons. The true feelings of the season can arrive earlier or later than the calendar indicates. It is up to you as a green witch to observe, trust, and choose to celebrate when you feel the season has truly arrived. Remember, the key to developing your own personal practice is forging your own connection with the energy flow of the year as it is influenced by the weather and climate where you live.

Summer Solstice:
Longest day

Spring and Autumn Equinoxes:
Day and night are equally long

Winter Solstice:
Shortest day

SOUTH   WEST

The seasonal tides echo the natural cycle in the inner life of the green witch:

Spring equinox to summer solstice ● the growing tide
Summer solstice to autumn equinox ● the reaping tide
Autumn equinox to winter solstice ● the resting tide
Winter solstice to spring equinox ● the cleansing tide

These four tides may be seen as stages of your life. The cyclic nature of life is reflected in your relationships and careers and what you learn as you grow. You can imagine it as a spiral. The energies of seasonal tides give the green witch opportunities to look inside themself and see all nature reflected in miniature there.

"By understanding how the year ebbs and flows, you gain a deeper understanding of how life itself weaves, unravels, and reweaves the web of life."

CELEBRATE the SEASONS

In your personal practice, observe how you feel for a year and base your own festivals on those observations. This is better than consulting a book, finding out that it is the fall equinox, reading that it is associated with endings and harvests, and then celebrating accordingly. What if you think of fall as a beginning? While celebrating the age-old associations can be positive and nurture a sense of unity with your ancestors and with the earth, it can also be counterintuitive if it does not coincide with the energies of your geographic locale. Honor the energies to which you are seeking to attune yourself. Celebrating the solstices and equinoxes involves allowing yourself to interact with the natural environment around you.

MEDITATIONS FOR EVERY SEASON

Meditating at each seasonal shift is one of the most direct ways of experiencing the energy of the natural world and tracing your own response to its ebb and flow throughout the year. Use the following seasonal meditation outline as the basis for your meditations. Appropriate seasonal variations (as listed in the section on each season later in this chapter) are given. Using a consistent meditation with only these small variations lets you easily sense the minor differences that come out of the meditation that you might otherwise miss if you followed a different sequence each time.

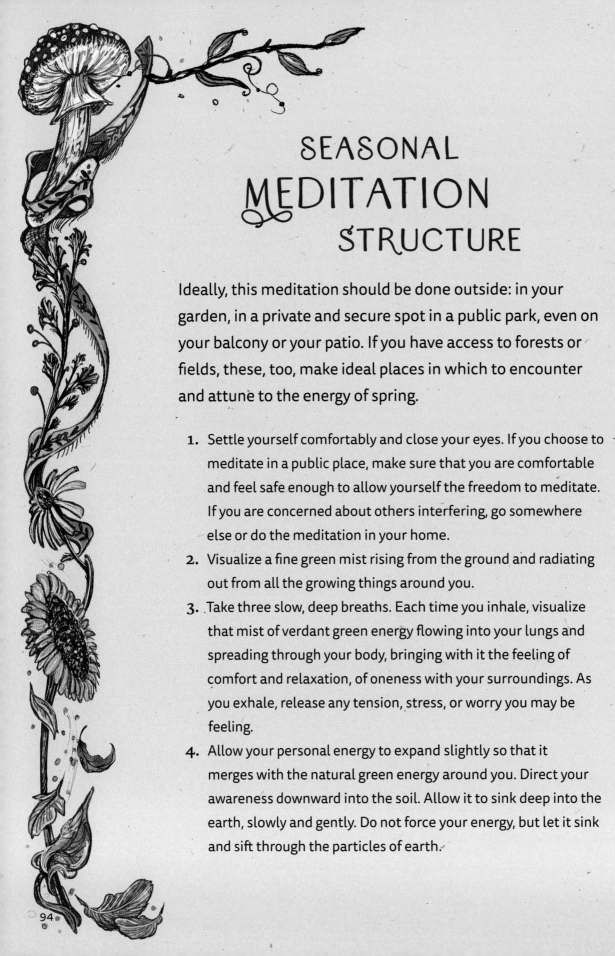

SEASONAL
MEDITATION
STRUCTURE

Ideally, this meditation should be done outside: in your garden, in a private and secure spot in a public park, even on your balcony or your patio. If you have access to forests or fields, these, too, make ideal places in which to encounter and attune to the energy of spring.

1. Settle yourself comfortably and close your eyes. If you choose to meditate in a public place, make sure that you are comfortable and feel safe enough to allow yourself the freedom to meditate. If you are concerned about others interfering, go somewhere else or do the meditation in your home.

2. Visualize a fine green mist rising from the ground and radiating out from all the growing things around you.

3. Take three slow, deep breaths. Each time you inhale, visualize that mist of verdant green energy flowing into your lungs and spreading through your body, bringing with it the feeling of comfort and relaxation, of oneness with your surroundings. As you exhale, release any tension, stress, or worry you may be feeling.

4. Allow your personal energy to expand slightly so that it merges with the natural green energy around you. Direct your awareness downward into the soil. Allow it to sink deep into the earth, slowly and gently. Do not force your energy, but let it sink and sift through the particles of earth.

5. When you feel comfortable, stop and feel the energy of the soil around you cradling you, enfolding you.

6. *Insert the appropriate seasonal visualization here.*

7. When you feel it is time to return to normal consciousness, offer the soil around your awareness a small gift of gratitude (emotion is energy, after all), then allow your awareness to slowly rise up through the soil to return to your physical body. After spending time within the earth like this, you will probably be so relaxed that slow movement will be natural to you. Make sure that you take the time to return thoroughly. Do not simply snap yourself back, or you will be disoriented and your personal energy will be unbalanced.

8. Once your awareness has returned, ground yourself (see Chapter 3) and take three deep breaths.

9. Open your eyes and gently move your arms and legs to warm them up and to reaffirm your physical form. Stand up slowly and do a few gentle stretches to loosen up your muscles. Write a summary of your experience in your green witch journal. How did it feel to interact with the earth at this season? Did the interaction teach you anything new? Did you learn anything new about your geographic location? Did you pick up any insight from the experience? Write down your thoughts and questions, any visions you may have had or new understandings you may have come to. Make notes on how you feel as this season begins, what the energy of the location you chose felt like. Remember to note the weather too.

THE SPRING EQUINOX

The movement of the seasons is a never-ending cycle. Although in reality there is no place that we can firmly point to as the beginning of the seasonal cycle, spring is often seen as the first season in the sequence. This comes from the fact that earlier calendars began the year in the spring. Spring is also traditionally associated with new beginnings, sowing, childhood, and young things in general. Spring is a time of potential, a time for planning and planting, and a time for making wishes about what you want the future to hold. The spring (or vernal) equinox takes place at the moment when night and day are of equal length for the first time after the winter solstice. From this moment on, the sun will be in the sky for a few more minutes every day, and nights will slowly become shorter.

Meditation

Spring Equinox

Perform this meditation on or around the spring equinox. If the day of the official equinox doesn't work for you, try it around the time of year when there are many new things emerging in the natural environment where you live.

1. Begin the meditation as outlined in the seasonal meditation structure.
2. Once you have reached a place of comfort deep inside the earth, breathe in that energy and feel it fill your body. Feel the soil's energy at this time of the spring equinox. Feel the potential that vibrates in the earth. Reach out and sense the first movements of roots and seeds where they curl in safety, absorbing the soil's energy and using it to nourish their own life force, growing stronger in their sleep. Sense the slow awakening of these roots and seeds, and think about the potential they hold and the luxurious life they will soon display.
3. Remain cradled by the energy of the soil as long as you like, enjoying the feeling of potential and the first stirrings of life.
4. Finish the meditation as outlined in the seasonal meditation structure.

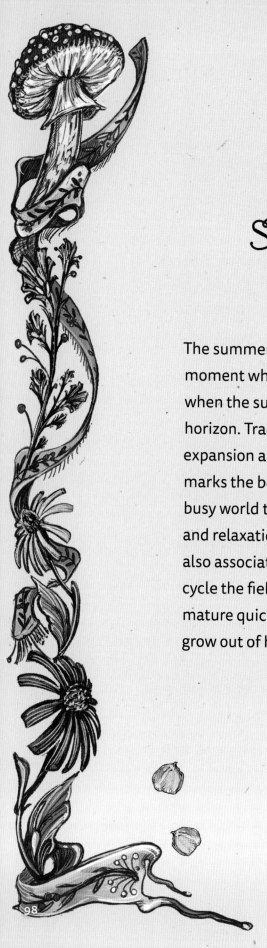

THE
SUMMER
SOLSTICE

The summer solstice, or midsummer, marks the moment when the sun is at its highest. It is the day when the sun spends the most hours above the horizon. Traditionally, this day is associated with expansion and great energy. The summer solstice marks the beginning of summer, a period in today's busy world that we nostalgically associate with play and relaxation and summer vacations. Conversely, it is also associated with hard work, for in the agricultural cycle the fields must be tended. Crops continue to mature quickly and with great strength and can easily grow out of hand.

Meditation

Summer Solstice

Perform this meditation on or around the summer solstice, or whenever you sense summer has arrived where you live. If this doesn't work for you, try it around another time of year when things are in the middle of a period of growth and expansion.

1. Begin the meditation as outlined in the previous seasonal meditation structure.
2. Once you have reached a place of comfort deep inside the earth, breathe that energy in and feel it fill your body.
3. Feel the soil's energy at this time of the summer solstice. Feel the energy of nourishment and growth that vibrates in the earth. Sense the expansion, the throb of life as it flows through roots and stems. Explore the interactive system of minerals, nutrients, water, and fertile decomposed vegetable matter that feeds the new generation of plant life. Sense the feeling of vitality, of life, of expansion and increase, of reaching up and opening out, the flow of passionate and joyful creation that pulses through the land.
4. Remain cradled by the energy of the soil as long as you like, enjoying the feeling of vitality and fertile life around you.
5. Finish the meditation as outlined in the seasonal meditation structure.

THE
AUTUMN
EQUINOX

As at the spring equinox, the minutes of day and night are precisely equal at the moment of the autumn equinox. From the summer solstice, the minutes of daylight have slowly decreased and the minutes of night have increased. Fall is traditionally associated with harvest and thanksgiving for the bounty of the earth, which has been tended from even before plants began to grow. Fall also incorporates themes of sacrifice, loss, and gentle regret, for the precious days of summer have passed and winter now approaches. Autumn is a time of weighing. What is necessary to keep? What can be left behind as the cycle passes to a time of scarcity?

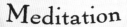

Meditation

Autumn Equinox

Perform this meditation on or around the autumn equinox or whenever you sense that fall has arrived where you live. Alternatively, try it around the time of year when things are in the middle of a period of fulfillment and harvest and nearing the end of their cycle.

1. Begin the meditation as outlined in the seasonal meditation structure.
2. Once you have reached a place of comfort deep inside the earth, breathe that energy in and feel it fill your body.
3. Feel the soil's energy at this time of the autumn equinox. Feel the energy of completion and contentment that vibrates in the earth. Reach out and sense the fullness, the feeling of achievement as it flows through roots and stems. Explore the gentle, slower movement of energy throughout the soil and the roots of plants as the cycle of producing fruit and seed comes to an end on the surface of the earth. Sense the feelings of contentment, of life, of pleasure and satisfaction, of appreciation and offering that pulse through the land.
4. Remain cradled by the energy of the soil as long as you like, enjoying the feeling of plenty and serenity around you.
5. Finish the meditation as outlined in the seasonal meditation structure.

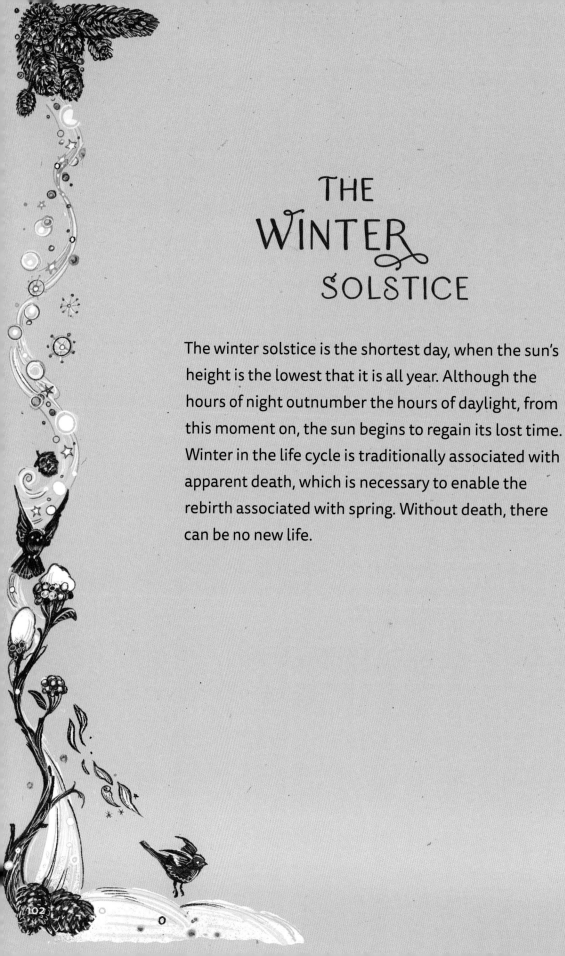

THE WINTER SOLSTICE

The winter solstice is the shortest day, when the sun's height is the lowest that it is all year. Although the hours of night outnumber the hours of daylight, from this moment on, the sun begins to regain its lost time. Winter in the life cycle is traditionally associated with apparent death, which is necessary to enable the rebirth associated with spring. Without death, there can be no new life.

Winter Solstice

Perform this meditation on or around the winter solstice, or whenever you sense that winter has arrived where you live. If this doesn't work for you, try it around the time of year when things have reached a point of rest, of apparent death or cessation of motion.

1. Begin the meditation as outlined in the previous seasonal meditation structure.
2. Once you have reached a place of comfort deep inside the earth, breathe that energy in and feel it fill your body.
3. Feel the soil's energy at this time of the winter solstice. Feel the energy of quiet and stillness that permeates the earth. Reach out and sense the darkness, the feeling of slowness as it flows through roots and stems. Explore the barely perceptible movement of energy throughout the soil and roots as the world above lies sleeping. Sense the feelings of relaxation, of incubation, of dreams and the breath of what may become that trickle through the land.
4. Remain cradled by the energy of the soil as long as you like, enjoying the feeling of warm stillness and sleep around you.
5. Finish the meditation as outlined in the seasonal meditation structure.

RITUALS FOR EVERY SEASON

Meditations are one method of interacting with the energy of the season. Rituals are another. Because green witchcraft is informal, whether to use the popular neopagan practice of creating a ritual circle to set the ritual site apart from the mundane world is up to the individual green witch. In occult traditions, the circle represents protection from negative forces that could interfere in your work. In the green witch's practice, however, those who choose to use a circle use it to designate an area of purity in which to work, a sacred place set apart for the ritual. If you choose to delineate your ritual area in this fashion, you may simply walk the perimeter of your space with the intent of marking it. No further formal action, visualization, or words are required.

The four seasons offer both

practical

and

spiritual

opportunities for learning more about nature and living in harmony with it. The beginnings of the four seasons are specific points at which to pause and evaluate your life.

Spend the day outdoors.

Go for a walk through your neighborhood and look at how things are changing.

Gather seasonal greenery and decorate your home.

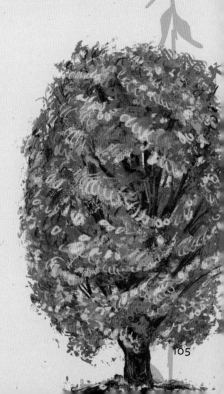

Spring Equinox Egg Ritual for Welcoming Creative Energy Into Your Life

This ritual is designed to gather up some of the abundant, fertile energy of nature in the springtime and direct it toward an area of your life where you could use a shot of productive, creative energy.

This spell appeals to the spring maiden and the youthful sun for their blessings and energy; it deliberately uses symbolic figures in this ritual so that you can visualize them as you desire.

Before beginning this spell, color your uncooked egg according to your personal color associations. For example, if the area of your life which requires energy is career related, you might color the egg brown or orange; if it is related to romance, you may wish to color the egg red or pink. Perform this ritual in your home at your altar, or wherever you feel comfortable.

YOU WILL NEED

Matches or a lighter

1 small, pale green candle

1 uncooked egg, colored according to your preference

Pen

Small piece of parchment

Heatproof dish

STEPS TO TAKE

1. Create sacred space however you prefer to do so.

2. Light the candle and take the egg into your hands. Say the following and then set the egg next to the candle:

> *Maiden Goddess of Spring, light, and life,*
> *Youthful God of the Sun, exuberant and joyful:*
> *Bless this egg, and fill it with the power of spring, of life,*
> *Of fertile and creative energy.*
> *May my life be energized!*

3. Using the pen, write on the parchment the situation or area of your life to which you wish to direct the creative energy of spring. When you have finished writing, hold the paper between your hands and empower it with your need.

4. Carefully touch the corner of the paper to the candle flame until it catches fire. Drop it in the heatproof dish and allow the paper to burn completely to ash.

5. Allow the candle to burn down completely. Let the egg rest beside the candle.

6. When the candle has gone out, take the egg and the bowl of ashes outdoors and dig a hole in the ground. Place the egg in the hole and sprinkle the ashes of the paper on top of it. Bury these carefully and with reverence. The energy of the egg and the earth will slowly begin to infuse the situation in your life that you asked to be energized.

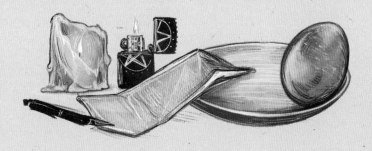

Summer Garden Blessing Ritual

Making flower chains is a wonderful way to combine play, work, and creativity. Take advantage of the abundant and luxurious energy of expansion and growth that manifests in the summertime to bless your garden with this ritual. Before you begin, select a place in your garden to serve as a place of offering. Gather the leaves and flowers you will be using from your garden or the wild (remembering to harvest responsibly); do not buy them from a florist. If you wish, use your hand instead of the staff or wand.

YOU WILL NEED

Wand or staff

Stang (forked staff or stick)

12 flowers (your choice; wildflowers and weeds are fine, but make sure the stems are at least 4 inches long and do not select anything with toxic leaves)

12 leaves (your choice; as large as possible, with firm stems)

Knife or scissors (optional)

Pitcher, bowl, cup, or watering can full of water

STEPS TO TAKE

1. With the wand or staff in your hand, circle around or walk through your garden. Hold the wand or staff in front of you, its base close to the ground. Visualize the life energy as it rises up from the soil through the plants' roots to nourish the stems, leaves, flowers, and fruit. Circle or walk through the garden a second time, still holding the wand or staff, but this time raised higher so that the tip reaches into the sky. Visualize the energy of the sun and the rain nourishing the plants from above.

2. Circle or walk through the garden a third and final time, now holding the wand or staff horizontally. Visualize the energy of each individual growing plant expanding to join with the other plants around it, forming the whole of your garden.

3. Lay down the wand or staff in front of your chosen place of offering. Take up the stang, and insert the single end into the earth firmly so that the forked end stands upright and stable.

4. Sit or kneel in front of the stang and take up one of the flowers. Strip away any leaves or greenery along the stem and trim it to approximately 4 inches long. With your fingernail (or the knife or scissors, if you prefer), make a small vertical slit in the stem about 1–2 inches below the petals. Don't make the slit too long; ½ inch ought to be enough. Do the same to the other eleven flowers.

5. Hold the first flower just below the petals. Pick up a second flower and carefully insert the end of the stem into the slit in the first flower. Carefully pull the stem of the second flower through the slit until the slit in the second stem has passed through the first stem's slit.

6. Pick up a third flower and insert its stem into the slit on the second flower. Repeat until all twelve flowers have been assembled into a chain.

7. Gently hang the flower chain on the stang by laying each end over one of the branches so that the middle of the chain forms a gentle swag. If the chain is not long enough, simply hang it over the fork itself.

8. In each of the leaves, make a tiny slit in the stem of the leaf.

9. Take one leaf and hold it in your hand. Take a second and gently insert the stem into the slit of the first leaf. Pull the second stem through until the slit passes through the first slit. Continue with the remaining leaves, until you have another chain.

continued

109

continued

10. Gently hang the leaf chain on the stang by laying each end over one of the branches, so that it lies along the flower chain. If the leaf chain is not long enough, simply hang it over the fork or gently twine it around the flower chain.

11. Lay both your hands on the chains and say:

> *Powers of Wind and Earth,*
> *Powers of Sun and Rain:*
> *By tree and flower and leaf,*
> *With my hands and heart,*
> *I bless this garden with life and love.*

12. Take up the pitcher or bowl of water and walk through your garden, gently sprinkling drops of the water throughout. Keep some water back. Return to the stang and pour the last of the water at its base where it has been thrust into the ground and say:

> *I give thanks to the earth for its bounty, its protection, and its support.*
> *Blessed be the earth and those who walk upon it.*

13. If you like, you can sit by the stang and meditate for a while or simply enjoy being in your garden. You can also weed, work the soil, thin out some plants, or do whatever gardening needs to be done. Leave the chains on the stang for at least a day (or as long as you feel right in leaving them). Remove them when they have wilted, but do not throw them out. Add them to your compost pile.

Autumn Equinox Harvest Ritual

This ritual honors the earth's produce and bounty and allows you to participate in the season's energy by performing the essential harvesting action. Harvest something from your own garden or something wild. If you have a lot to harvest, choose the first or the last item you plan to harvest for this ritual. The harvesting tool will depend on what you are harvesting.

YOU WILL NEED

Sharp knife, secateurs, scissors, or shears

Small bottle or bowl of water

STEPS TO TAKE

1. Standing next to what you are harvesting, reach out with your hand and sense that plant's energy. Say:

> *I honor you, earth's child.*
> *I honor your growth, your flower, and now your fruit.*
> *I thank you for your energy.*
> *Blessed be, earth's child.*
> *May I who harvest your fruit be blessed by the act.*

2. With the harvesting tool, cut the fruit off the plant. Sense the energy of the plant when you have harvested its produce. Honor the difference you feel.

3. Pour the water at the base of the plant in thanks.

Ice Ritual for the Winter Solstice

This ritual is a physical reminder that spring will always follow winter. If you live in a region with no snow, make a batch of ice cubes prior to the ritual and use those. A metal bowl is recommended because it will best reflect the candle's flame, although it will grow very cold, so be aware of your fingers when you hold it. If it's wintry cold where you live, perform this ritual indoors. Otherwise, the ice and snow will not melt, and the point of the ritual will be lost. Perform this ritual in your home at your altar or wherever you feel comfortable.

YOU WILL NEED

Ice cubes or chunks of ice and snow from outdoors (around 1 cup)

Bowl (preferably metal)

Candle (red, orange, or yellow) in candleholder

Matches or a lighter

STEPS TO TAKE

1. Place the ice cubes or snow in the bowl and sit or kneel next to it. Light the candle and place it behind the bowl so that you can see the flame's reflection dancing in the ice or snow.

2. Say:

> As the season turns, and the sun shines,
> I hail the light that returns to the land.
> Darkness ebbs, light again flows,
> And day by day the land will grow warm.
> Welcome again, bright sun!
> May your beams caress the land and transform ice to water,
> Snow to rain, cold to warmth,
> And winter to spring again.

3. Allow the ice or snow to melt until it is water. Look at the reflection of the candle flame on the water in the bowl and think about the warmth of the sun. Feel the energy of the snow as it melts, the energy of the flame as it emits light and heat. Observe the communication between the two.

4. When you are finished, pour the water outside at the base of a tree.

CHAPTER 5

LIVE CLOSELY
with the
EARTH

he sources of the green witch's information, wisdom, and power are the different aspects of nature and the natural system—the luminaries in the sky above, the plant world, the mineral world. Using the bounty of nature in a personal spiritual practice offers the reward of knowledge and insight acquired through experience. This chapter looks at how the green witch uses the various elements of nature, including trees, flowers, herbs, and stones.

THE MAGIC of TREES

Trees are the pillars of our world. They anchor our ground and seem to hold up the sky. They form the backbone of the green witch's practice. While we tend to focus on herbs, we also work with wood, often when something more physically stable or permanent is required. The green witch's staff and stang, for example, are made of wood, as is the more traditional witch's tool, the wand. Sticks and twigs form the basis of many protective amulets, as do rounds cut from the cross-section of branches and inscribed with symbols. Wood is also used to build homes and furniture.

The parts of trees that you may use include bark, leaves, and inner wood. Here are the magical associations of common trees:

Apple

Ash

Cedar

Birch

Elder

Apple *Pyrus malus*

Apple trees are found all over the Northern Hemisphere. Their widespread availability and fertile abundance bring to mind their association with life, longevity, and fertility. Magically, apple trees are associated with love, healing, harmony, and longevity.

Ash *Fraxinus excelsior*

Ash is one of the trees considered by some European cultures to be the World Tree. Magically, ash is associated with water, strength, intellect, willpower, protection, justice, balance and harmony, skill, travel, weather, and wisdom.

Birch *Betula spp.*

The traditional witch's broom is made of birch twigs. Magically, birch is associated with cleansing, protection, and purification. It is also associated with children; cradles were often made of birch wood.

Cedar *Thuja occidentalis* —YELLOW CEDAR; *Juniperus virginiana* —RED CEDAR

A precious wood that is recognized by many cultures as magical and powerful, cedar has been known throughout the ages for its protective qualities as well as its ability to repel insects and pests. With its aromatic scent, cedar was often given as an offering. Magically, cedar is associated with healing, spirituality, purification, protection, prosperity, and harmony.

Elder *Sambucus canadensis, Sambucus nigra*

Elder is also known as witchwood. It is said that bad luck will fall upon anyone who does not ask the tree's permission three times before harvesting any part of it. Medicinally, elder bark is used as a diuretic, purgative, and emetic. The berries are used as a laxative and diuretic and also induce perspiration, and the leaves are used as an external emollient for irritated skin, sprains, and bruises. An infusion of elderflowers taken as a tea stimulates perspiration, thus helping the body to work through a cold or illness, and also helps loosen chest and sinus congestion. Magically, elder wood is associated with protection (especially against being struck by lightning), prosperity, and healing.

Hawthorn
Crataegus oxyacantha

The hawthorn shrub was often used as a boundary marker. In fact, haw is an old word for "hedge." If hawthorn grows together with an oak and ash tree, it is said that the fairy folk can be seen among the trees. Even where it grows alone, hawthorn is considered to be a fairy favorite. Like oak, the hawthorn produces hard wood and great heat when burned. Magical associations include fertility, harmony, happiness, the otherworld, and protection.

Hazel *Corylus avellana*

The hazel tree has long been associated in European folklore with wisdom. Gods and mythological figures associated with the hazel include Thor, Brigid, and Apollo. The nuts and branches are used for magic, and the hazel is associated with luck, fertility, protection, and wish granting.

Honeysuckle
Lonicera caprifolium, Lonicera periclymenum

Also known as woodbine or hedge-tree, the honeysuckle is associated with liminal or transitional states. The scent of honeysuckle flowers is strongest in the evening. Magical associations include psychic awareness, harmony, healing, prosperity, and happiness.

Lilac *Syringa spp.*

Beautiful springtime flowers with a sweet, full scent can be used to make floral water and flavored sugar. Lilacs are associated with protection, beauty, love, psychic abilities, purification, and prosperity.

Maple *Acer spp.*

Maple is another popular tree used for cabinetry and by artisans. It is also a source of dye and maple sugar. Magically, maple is used for love, prosperity, life and health, and general abundance.

Oak *Quercus robur*

Oak is magically associated with defense, thunder, strength, courage, healing, longevity, protection, and good fortune. Because the wood is very strong and durable, oak has been used in home construction and in shipbuilding. The bark is used to tan leather and as a dye. Acorns, the fruit of the oak tree, are symbols of fertility. When found growing in oak trees, mistletoe was considered to be particularly potent by the druids and was important in their magical work.

Hawthorn

Hazel

Honeysuckle

Lilac

Maple

Oak

Pine

Rowan

Poplar

Willow

Witch Hazel

Yew

Pine *Pinus spp.*

Popularly used in building, the pine is one of the most common trees in North America. Its resin is used for the creation of turpentine and soaps, and for the production of rosin. Amber, one of the most beloved gems for magical jewelry, is fossilized pine sap. Magically, pine is used for cleansing and purification, healing, clarity of mind, prosperity, and protection from evil.

Poplar *Populus spp.*

Also known as aspen, poplar's magical associations include prosperity, communication, exorcism, and purification.

Rowan *Pyrus aucuparia, Sorbus aucuparia*

Rowan is also known as quicken, hornbeam, witchwood, and mountain ash. Rowan berries have been used in brewing, and the bark has been used for tanning and as a dye. Magical associations include improving psychic powers, divination, healing, protection from evil, peace, creativity, success, and change and transformation.

Willow *Salix alba*

The white willow, (or weeping willow), has long, flexible branches. Associated with the moon, the willow has an affinity for water and is often found growing near it. In folklore, the willow is associated with the Goddess and feminine cycles. Because it easily recovers from trauma, willow is also associated with growth and renewal. Magical associations of willow include love, tranquility, harmony, protection, and healing.

Witch Hazel *Hamamelis virginiana*

Also known as snapping hazelnut, for the spontaneous cracking open of its seedpods, witch hazel has long been used as a poultice for bruises and swellings. Witch hazel extracts are used for their astringent properties. Magical associations include protection, healing, and peace.

Yew *Taxus baccata*

Yew is poisonous, which may be one of the reasons it is so closely associated with death. The yew produces a very hard wood and was used where construction required an unyielding, inflexible structure. Magically, it is associated with spirits and the otherworld.

Ritual

Tree Attunement Exercise

Before you begin, refresh your memory on sensing energy techniques in Chapter 3.

1. Pick a tree. Stand next to it. Hold one hand about 1 inch away from the bark. Extend your awareness and feel the energy of the tree. After you've finished this exercise, make notes about your observations in your journal.

2. With the same tree, touch the bark. Explore how the tree feels to your hands. Bend close and smell the tree. Close your eyes and listen to the sounds the tree makes in response to the environment. Look closely at the tree and see the different textures, colors, and markings. If it has fruit and you know it to be safe, taste it. Make notes in your journal.

3. Conduct these exercises with different kinds of trees. Compare and contrast your experiences.

4. Do these exercises with different trees of the same genus. What are the similarities between the trees? What are the differences?

FLOWERS

Most plants flower in some way; it's part of the natural cycle. Even plants you might not expect to flower do, albeit briefly or at long intervals, like cacti or succulents. When we think of flowers, however, we often mean a plant that is grown specifically for its blossoms. The flower of a plant carries a tidy bundle of energy, for it is the sexual organ of the plant, part of how the plant reproduces.

COLOR MEANINGS

Color carries its own energy, and so the color of a flower can subtly modify the plant's energies. Over time, different colors have been associated with different magical goals, and a list is included here for reference. However, your own personal associations with the plant, including its color, will influence your work with them.

Here's a basic list of color correspondences:

Red
life, passion, action, energy

Pink
affection, friendship

Orange
success, speed, career, action

Yellow
intellectual matters, communication

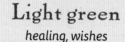

Light green
healing, wishes

Dark green
prosperity, money, nature

Light blue
truth, spirituality, tranquility, peace

Dark blue
healing, justice

Violet
mysticism, meditation, spirituality

Purple
occult power, spirituality

Black
protection, fertility, mystery

Brown
stability, home, career

White
purity, psychic development

COMMON FLOWERS

Flowers can be grown for color, scent, and food, besides aesthetic pleasure. The energy they carry can be subtly different from the stalks or leaves; try working with each to see which energy you prefer. Flowers are part of the reproductive system of a plant, attracting pollinators who mix pollen from different plants as they travel. Once fertilized, seeds develop in the ovary portion of the flower. For this reason, flowers in general can be used for fertility or abundance magic.

Here are some flowers commonly found in a green witch's garden.

Calendula
Calendula officinalis

Magically associated with protection, psychic abilities, dreams, success with legal issues, fidelity, healing, love, animals, and comfort.

How to Grow: Commonly known as pot marigolds, calendula is a hardy plant that can tolerate a wide range of light conditions, from lower light to full sun. They thrive in beds or containers but prefer cooler weather. The plants bloom throughout the growing season and will bloom more than once if you cut off older flowers. Provide regular water and a balanced fertilizer for best results.

Carnation
Dianthus spp.

The carnation has a wonderful healing energy and makes an excellent gift for the sick. Carnations are used magically for protection, strength, energy, luck, and healing.

How to Grow: Carnations can tolerate a wide range of conditions. These free-flowering plants prefer soil that is slightly alkaline (like most plants) and will grow in containers or beds, forming low mounds that will bloom most heavily in the spring. Beware that Dianthus species may be toxic to pets, so if you're growing them inside keep the plant away from curious animals.

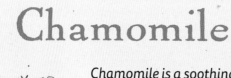

Chamomile
Chamaemelum nobile, Matricaria chamomilla

Chamomile is a soothing, calming herb, both when taken as an infused tea and when worked with magically. Chamomile is magically associated with money, love, sleep, meditation, purification, protection, and tranquility.

How to Grow: Members of the daisy family, these pretty and small flowers add a wildflower look wherever they are planted. They prefer to grow in full sun in well-drained (not soggy) beds or containers. Chamomile flowers appear in large numbers in the early midsummer and will continuously bloom until fall.

Daffodil *Narcissus spp.*

The daffodil is an excellent flower to use in charms for love and charms for fertility. Magically, the daffodil is associated with luck, fertility, and love.

How to Grow: These bulbs should be planted in the fall, before frost and snow. In the spring, the young daffodils will send up blooms, one of the early signs of a new growing season. Daffodils do best with bright or full sun to encourage blooming. Avoid planting them in soggy, low-lying areas where the bulbs may rot. Plant your bulbs with the pointed end facing up, about 3–6 inches apart.

Daisy *Leucanthemum vulgare, Chrysanthemum leucanthemum*

Also known as field daisy and oxeye daisy, the daisy is commonly associated with love and flirtation. Magically, the daisy is associated with love, hope, and innocence. Use the daisy in magic associated with children as well.

How to Grow: These yellow and white flowering perennials like to grow in full sun, or in slight shade to protect from midday sun, in beds of well-drained soil. Daisies cannot tolerate standing water, so make sure your growing area has plenty of drainage. Deadhead the flowers to encourage more blooms, and replace the plants every two or three years to keep them vibrant.

Gardenia *Gardenia spp.*

Gardenia attracts tranquil energy to a place or individual. Gardenia is also used in love spells and charms. Magically, gardenia is associated with harmony, healing, love, and peace.

How to Grow: Gardenias are known for their creamy white flowers and evocative early evening scent. These subtropical or tropical shrubs prefer rich, organic soil that is slightly acidic, so use a specially formulated fertilizer for acid-loving plants. They do well in partly shaded conditions, but they are susceptible to sooty mold and fungus, so avoid drenching the foliage.

Geranium *Pelargonium spp.*

Grown indoors or out, geraniums carry strong protective energy and extend this energy through the area around them. Rose geranium is used in love spells. Magically, geraniums are associated with fertility, love, healing, courage, and protection.

How to Grow: These plants excel as bedding plants, in container gardens, or in hanging baskets (encourage more blooms by snipping off dead flowers). Geraniums like slightly acidic soil and thrive in a rich, organic planting medium with plenty of regular water. Be aware that geraniums are toxic to both humans and animals.

Hyacinth *Muscari racemosum, Hyacinthus non-scriptus*

Both grape and wild hyacinths have a lovely spring-like scent. Hyacinths bloom for a short period, but produce a vibrant energy. Hyacinths are magically associated with love, happiness, and protection.

How to Grow: Hyacinths are the harbingers of spring and signal the start of a new growing season. After the blooms begin to fade, snip them off. This prevents seed formation and preserves the bulb's strength for another growing season. If seedpods form, remove them. Plant bulbs in the fall in a sunny spot.

Iris *Iris florentina*

Irises are a spring flower magically used for purification and blessing as well as wisdom. The three petals symbolize faith, wisdom, and valor. The root is called orris root, and when ground up it produces a mildly sweet powder used for peace, harmony, and love.

How to Grow: These flowering plants grow from rhizomes, or underground stems, that are planted in a sunny location in sandy, very well-drained soil. They are heavy feeders that require a good dose of fertilizer in the early spring to perform best. Every few years, dig up and divide the rhizomes to give new plants more room and increase your stock.

Jasmine *Jasminum spp.*

Jasmine possesses a heady but delicate scent that is usually stronger at night. Because of this, it is often associated with the moon and feminine energy. Magically, jasmine is associated with love, meditation, spirituality, harmony, and prosperity.

How to Grow: There are multiple kinds of jasmine, and the most popular varieties reward their gardeners with a beautiful scent. Jasmine is available as a vine or a shrub or even a small tree. They can be grown indoors in containers or outside on trellises or as border plants. Jasmine should be grown in full or partial sun, in a warm location with well-drained soil.

Lavender *Lavandula spp.*

Lavender is used frequently in magical and non-magical applications. Thanks to its gentle scent, it is an ideal herb to use in conjunction with magic for children, for it encourages relaxation and sleep. Magically, lavender is associated with peace, harmony, tranquility, love, purification, and healing.

How to Grow: With its soft leaves and purple flowers, lavender is a beloved member of the mint family. Suitable for containers or massed beds, lavender prefers full sun and well-drained, even slightly drier soil. The plants bloom in midsummer with masses of small purple flowers on graceful, small stalks. They are toxic to animals.

Lilac *Syringa vulgaris*

The sweet, wild scent of lilacs in late spring is a heady experience. The flowers of this shrub are usually white or shades of purple. Magically, they are used for protection and banishing negative energy.

How to Grow: Grown as hedges or informal bushes, lilacs bloom with large clusters of flowers in a variety of colors. Some varieties of lilac can reach up to 30 feet at maturity, but dwarf varieties are generally under 10 feet. Lilacs appreciate plenty of organic material in the soil and are considered low-maintenance shrubs.

Lily *Lilium spp.*

Lilies are associated with protection and the elimination of hexes. In some cultures, lilies are associated with the concept of death and the afterlife.

How to Grow: Lilies are grown from bulbs as perennial flowers that emerge in spring and bloom in the early summer or fall. Plant lily bulbs in the fall, before the ground freezes. Plant them about three times as deep as the height of the bulb, pointed side facing up, about 15–18 inches apart. After the bloom is finished, cut off the flower stalk but do not remove old leaves until they are dead in the fall.

Lily *of the* Valley
Convallaria magalis

This tiny cascade of white or cream-colored bell-shaped flowers has a delicate scent. Magically, it enhances concentration and mental ability and is used to encourage happiness.

How to Grow: Lily of the valley is a popular perennial ground cover in shady or semi-shady conditions, such as under trees. These spreading, low plants are tough and can easily take over a bed once they're established. Fertilize in the spring and provide regular watering for best results. These plants are very toxic to people and animals alike.

Lupine *Lupinus spp.*

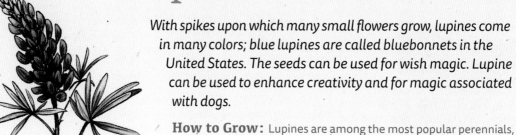

With spikes upon which many small flowers grow, lupines come in many colors; blue lupines are called bluebonnets in the United States. The seeds can be used for wish magic. Lupine can be used to enhance creativity and for magic associated with dogs.

How to Grow: Lupines are among the most popular perennials, beloved for their dramatic flower spikes. They do best planted in sandy, very well-drained soil with regular watering and cooler temperatures. Deadhead your lupines to encourage more blooms, and feed them regularly throughout the summer months. Start your lupine garden by spreading seeds in the spring or transplanting seedlings.

Pansy *Viola tricolor*

The pansy is a hardy, cheerful-looking plant with multicolored flowers related to the violet. It blooms throughout the summer and comes in both annual and perennial varieties. Magically, it is used for divination, communication, happiness, and love.

How to Grow: Pansies are very popular and delicate flowering plants that like cooler temperatures and will suffer in hotter climates or heat spells. Plants bloom in the spring and early summer and are usually grown as annuals. They prefer very well-drained soil in full sun to partial shade and do best with lots of fertilizer.

Poppy *Papaver rhoeas*

Also known as the corn poppy, the red poppy is a bright flower with a furry stem and leaves. Poppy seeds are used in cooking and baking. Magically, the poppy is associated with tranquility, fertility, prosperity, love, sleep, and invisibility.

How to Grow: Red poppies are great for wildflower gardens. These flowers offer up delicate cup-shaped red blooms in the spring and summer. Poppies are known as low-maintenance plants that tolerate a wide range of light exposure and soil conditions. Remove older flowers to encourage blooming. Red poppies are toxic to pets.

Primrose *Primula vulgaris*

The primrose is most commonly pale yellow, although white and pale pink species exist. They are a favorite of pollinators. Primroses are good for magic associated with children, protection, and new beginnings. They can be a nice addition to rites of passage.

How to Grow: Primroses are early spring bloomers that grow as a low ground cover in partly shaded areas. Primroses prefer cooler temperatures to germinate. The plants themselves are not demanding—they like average water and temperature and aren't picky about their preferred soil type.

Rose *Rosa spp.*

Folklore and literature have made the rose synonymous with love. The flower has a gentle scent, the intensity of which varies from species to species. Magically, the rose is associated with healing, divination, tranquility, harmony, psychic ability, and protection.

How to Grow: Roses have a reputation as difficult plants. Many roses grow easily, however; check your local garden center for which varieties will thrive in your environment. Roses grow as small, spiky shrubs in full sun. They like plenty of water in well-drained soil. Feed regularly to encourage their blooms, which appear in spring or summer.

Snapdragon *Antirrhinum majus*

Snapdragons have a lovely innocent energy. Magically, they are used for protection, particularly from illusion or deception, or to reflect negative energy to its source. Plant snapdragons along the perimeter of your garden to protect it.

How to Grow: Snapdragons are technically perennials that are typically treated as annuals in cooler-region gardens. They are also very popular container and window box plants. Mature plants can range in size from a few inches up to 4 feet tall. They like full sun but will grow in partial shade. Snapdragons like soil with plenty of organic material, regular watering, and an early-season dose of fertilizer. Flowers will appear throughout the growing season.

Sunflower *Helianthus spp.*

The sunflower is associated with the sun and its energy, which means it carries magical associations of happiness, success, and health. The plant's abundant seeds carry the magical associations of fertility. Sunflowers are excellent in a summer solstice ritual. Germinate the seeds and then plant them to increase the energy of abundance in your garden in general.

How to Grow: These striking plants feature large flowers on tall stalks that may need to be staked up if the flower heads get too heavy. Sunflowers like light, moisture, and fertilizer—they don't like dry conditions and will turn brown in droughts.

Tulip *Tulipa spp.*

The chalice or cuplike shape of the tulip makes this flower ideal for use in prosperity and abundance magic. The tulip is also associated with protection, love, and happiness.

How to Grow: Tulips are a popular spring bulb that sends up delicate cupped flowers early in the growing season. Tulips have been extensively bred over the centuries to be available in a staggering array of colors. Tulips really shine when planted in massed beds, so their blooms will provide a bright splash of color in the garden while the other plants are still getting established. Tulip bulbs like rich soil and plenty of moisture. They do best in full sun.

Violet *Viola odorata*

The violet is a delicate flower used for peace, hope, harmony, protection, luck, love, sleep, and tranquility. Use violet in charms and sachets designed to maintain tranquility and to encourage peace. Violet also has aspects of fertility and abundance.

How to Grow: Violets are perennial plants that have been grown in Europe and Asia for hundreds of years. Commonly used as a ground cover, violets offer up small foliage and intensely fragrant flowers in the spring. They can thrive in light conditions ranging from full sun to partial shade with regular water and fertilizer. Violets spread by underground roots but are easy to control.

Flower Bowl for Summer Solstice

Making a flower bowl is a lovely way to celebrate the energies of high summer, when everything is in the full throes of expanding. For this bowl, choose flowers that bloom around the summer solstice in your region, preferably native ones. If you don't have access to any, you can buy some, choosing types that carry summer associations for you. Clip the flowers off the stems, leaving enough stem so that the head keeps together. If you prefer, or if it's easier, carefully separate petals to float them independently.

How many flowers you need will depend on the size of the bowl you use. Choose however many flowers that will fit floating around the edge of the bowl, as the center will be taken up by the glass and candle; you can crowd them or place them as sparsely as you choose.

This bowl also calls for amber (associated with the sun and health), carnelian (success), citrine (creativity), and malachite (earth and fertility) stones.

YOU WILL NEED

Glass or cup

Bowl

Spring water (or tap water that has sat for a day in sunlight or moonlight)

Tea light or votive candle in candleholder

Amber, carnelian, citrine, and malachite stones

Flowers blooming in your region around the summer solstice

Matches or a lighter

STEPS TO TAKE

1. Place the glass upside down in the bowl, so the flat bottom is up.
2. Pour the water in carefully. If the bowl is deep enough, you may have to allow some water under the glass so that it doesn't move. Don't fill the bowl completely; halfway is enough.
3. Place the tea light or votive candle on top of the reversed glass.
4. Add the stones to the water in the bowl, in whatever pattern or placement you like.
5. Float the flowers or petals on top of the water around the candle on the glass.
6. Light the candle and say:

> *Spirits of summer, bless this place and those within it.*
> *I honor your light and warmth, your burgeoning growth and expansion.*

7. Place the bowl outside in your garden (safely, away from dry plant matter; a burning candle should always be attended), on your altar, or in the heart of your home.

Notes: This is a lovely ritual to do with a cauldron, if you have one. For a larger container like that, use a jar candle to place in the center, such as a seven-day candle (also known as a novena or vigil candle). If doing this activity with a group, have everyone bring a stone to add and a flower to float in the water.

"Being active in nature
is important,

but it's equally important

to stop

and

to listen

to what it has to tell you. "

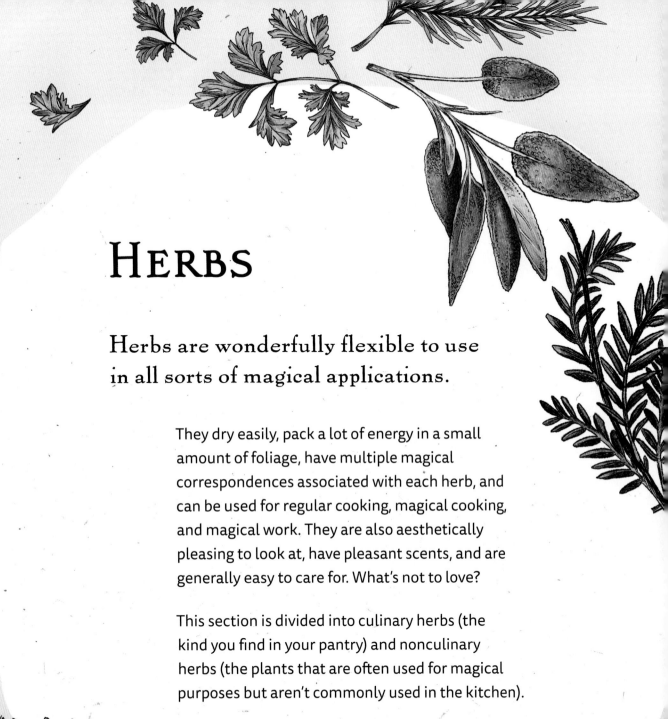

HERBS

Herbs are wonderfully flexible to use in all sorts of magical applications.

They dry easily, pack a lot of energy in a small amount of foliage, have multiple magical correspondences associated with each herb, and can be used for regular cooking, magical cooking, and magical work. They are also aesthetically pleasing to look at, have pleasant scents, and are generally easy to care for. What's not to love?

This section is divided into culinary herbs (the kind you find in your pantry) and nonculinary herbs (the plants that are often used for magical purposes but aren't commonly used in the kitchen).

COMMON CULINARY HERBS

ANGELICA *Angelica archangelica*

Also known as angel's herb, this fragrant plant has been used throughout the centuries for improving digestion, flavoring wines and liqueurs, and making candy. Magically, it is particularly powerful when used for protection and purification.

How to Grow: Angelica is not difficult to grow. Angelica blooms after two years of growth. Once done blooming, the plant will frequently die. Angelica likes somewhat cooler areas, so if you live in a hot area plant your angelica in a location that gets protection from the hottest sun. Always make sure your angelica gets plenty of water—it is sensitive to drought.

BASIL *Ocimum basilicum*

Also known as sweet basil and St. Joseph's Wort, basil is commonly found all over Europe and the Americas. It is versatile in the culinary arts and is an excellent all-purpose magical herb as well. Basil is used for prosperity, success, peace, protection, happiness, purification, and love.

How to Grow: Basil is one of the most rewarding herbs to grow because it's so vigorous. Basil prefers warmth, plenty of water, and lots of rich, organic soil. It does equally well in the ground or in containers, and you can start to harvest your basil as soon as it's established (younger basil is less likely to be bitter). Basil prefers 6–8 hours of sunlight every day.

BAY *Laurus nobilis*

Also known as sweet bay and sweet laurel. Bay is magically associated with success, wisdom, and divination. Write a wish on a bay leaf and sleep with it under your pillow for dreams that offer guidance as to how to pursue your goal.

How to Grow: Bay is a hardy shrub or even a small tree whose leaves are harvested and dried. Plant bay in a container or locate in a sunny location. Bay is only hardy in USDA hardiness zone 8 or higher, so in colder climates move the bay plant inside in winter. Bay likes well-drained soil, but thanks to a shallow root system the plant is sensitive to drought and should be watered regularly.

CARAWAY *Carum carvi*

The seed of the caraway plant is excellent to use for protection against negativity. It's also a good antitheft herb, so add some to sachets or charms in your home. Magical associations include health, mental abilities, protection, fidelity, and antitheft.

How to Grow: Caraway is frequently grown from seed, with gardeners sowing seeds in shallow holes about ¼ inch deep in the early spring. Caraway likes plenty of light and rich soil. Mature plants are about 3 feet tall and will bear seed the second year after planting. To harvest your caraway for seed, snip the plants when the fruit is ripe and then dry and separate the seeds from the pods.

CHIVES *Allium schoenoprasum*

The smallest of the onion family, chives have a delicate oniony taste that isn't overwhelming. The flowers are also edible. Like onions, they excel at protection and absorbing negative energy.

How to Grow: Chives are easy to grow in either a container or in a garden bed. Chives will do well in full sun. Chives like regular watering and plenty of fertilizer to perform best. If you're planting outside, separate your chive clumps after a few years to increase your plant stock and encourage new shoots. Chive leaves can be harvested as soon as they are large enough to snip away.

CINNAMON *Cinnamomum spp.*

Cinnamon possesses a great amount of energy. Add a pinch to anything to rev up the power level. It is excellent for money spells. Magically, cinnamon is associated with action, healing, protection, energy, love, and purification.

How to Grow: Cinnamon is harvested from the bark of cinnamon trees. Unless you live in a tropical climate, cinnamon should only be grown indoors so you can provide the heat, humidity, and bright light that cinnamon prefers. Cinnamon bark is ready to harvest when plants reach three years of age, when it's possible to peel away the outer bark and get to the yellow interior bark that is dried and ground.

DILL *Anethum graveolens*

Also known as dillweed, dill comes in two forms: seed and weed, which is the feathery dried leaves of the plant. Either may be used in green witch work. Dill is magically used for good fortune, tranquility, prosperity, lust, and protection.

How to Grow: Dill is a relatively easy herb to grow. For best results, plant your dill seeds in a sunny location. Provide steady water, but don't let your dill plant sit in water. Dill will set seeds in hot weather, so you can harvest the seeds as soon as the blooms have faded. To harvest dill, cut the entire plant at the stem and hang it upside down in a brown paper bag—the seeds will fall from the flowers.

MINT *Mentha spp.*

There is a wide variety of green or garden mints. An infusion of the leaves will help ease most headaches, stimulate the appetite, and aid digestion. Magical associations are prosperity, joy, fertility, purification, love, and success.

How to Grow: Mint plants are vigorous perennials that grow in a wide variety of conditions. In fact, mint is so easy to grow it's known for taking over whole gardens. Mint loves plenty of moisture but doesn't like boggy or soggy ground and will thrive in all kinds of light conditions, from full sun to dappled shade. Keep your mint varieties well watered, and you'll be rewarded with a steady supply of leaves.

NUTMEG *Myristica fragrans*

Medicinally, nutmeg quells nausea and soothes digestive problems (although it can be toxic in large doses). Magically, it is associated with psychic abilities, happiness, love, money, and health.

How to Grow: Nutmeg is harvested from trees that grow in tropical regions. In their native environment, nutmeg trees can grow to almost 100 feet and begin bearing fruit after about six years of growth. Nutmeg doesn't do well in containers, so you should only attempt to grow nutmeg if you live in a subtropical climate and have room for a full-sized tree.

PARSLEY *Petroselinum crispum*

In ancient Greece, parsley was used for such varied purposes as sprinkling on corpses to neutralize the smell of decay and making victors' crowns to celebrate success. It is magically associated with power, strength, purification, and prosperity. Both the seeds and the leaves can be used.

How to Grow: Hardy throughout much of North America, parsley can be grown in garden plots outdoors or in containers on your windowsill. Parsley likes a bright spot with plenty of water, but the well-mannered plants are relatively slow-growing and won't spread far. Harvest parsley when the plant reaches about 6 inches in height, cutting stems as needed.

ROSEMARY *Rosmarinus officinalis*

Practical applications of rosemary include use as a skin tonic applied externally and as a hair rinse to soothe an itchy scalp. An infusion taken as a tea will help ease a headache. Magical associations include protection, improving memory, wisdom, health, and healing.

How to Grow: Rosemary is a hardy evergreen shrub that is often grown as an ornamental plant as well as a culinary or magical herb. Rosemary does best in sunny locations that provide plenty of warmth. The plant is drought tolerant, so don't overwater your rosemary, and it responds well to pruning.

SAGE *Salvia spp.*

Sage is perhaps the herb most commonly used for purification and protection. An infusion taken as a tea will help settle a sour stomach and ease digestion and can help calm anxiety as well. Magical associations include purification and protection, wisdom, health, and long life.

How to Grow: Sage thrives in containers as well as in regular garden beds. Sage plants like full sun, but if you live in a warmer climate with strong sun, consider providing later-afternoon shade to protect your plant from the harshest sun. Sage plants should be allowed to grow unchecked for a season before you start harvesting leaves. Once the plant is mature, you can harvest leaves as needed.

TARRAGON *Artemisia dracunculus*

This herb can be used to enhance confidence, strength, and protection. It can remove negative energy, and promote emotional healing. Medicinally, tarragon tea can be used to promote recovery from illness and settle digestive issues.

How to Grow: Tarragon is a vigorous herb that does well in sunny areas. The plant tends to develop vigorous roots, so it's somewhat more drought tolerant than many herbs and can even grow in sandy soil. Adding a layer of mulch or other soil cover will make your tarragon even more hardy. Harvest leaves as soon as the plant is established.

THYME *Thymus vulgaris*

Used magically for protection and courage, thyme also can be used medicinally for sore throats. The oil has antiseptic properties, and can repel pests; add a few drops to a cup of water and spray it to keep creepy-crawlies away. Magically, it can help ease grief, uplift your mood, and deter negative energy.

How to Grow: Thyme thrives in full sunlight in a well-drained container or garden patch. Thyme has a reputation as being somewhat drought tolerant, so err on the side of less water. Thyme isn't picky about fertilizer, and it likes heat. Thyme is a perennial, so harvesting will encourage the plant to become fuller and more vigorous.

VERBENA *Verbena officinalis, Verbena spp.*

Also known as vervain, verbena is an excellent all-purpose herb. Magically versatile, verbena is associated with divination, protection, love, peace, tranquility, healing, prosperity, and reversal of negative activity. Add to any charm bag or spell to encourage success.

How to Grow: Verbena is a perennial herb that is grown as an annual in cooler regions. It thrives in containers. Verbena likes full sun and well-drained soil. It's sensitive to being overwatered. Regular fertilizer helps the plant achieve its mature size faster.

"The amount of personal energy infused in a plant that you have cared for as it grows and develops helps key it to your magical work later."

Nonculinary Herbs

COMFREY *Symphytum officinale*

Also known as boneset or knitbone, comfrey is renowned as a healing herb. Magically, it is associated with health, healing, protection during travel, and prosperity.

How to Grow: Comfrey is a highly adaptable perennial. The plant likes at least a few hours of full sunlight every day and isn't picky about the soil conditions as long as there is good drainage and regular water. Mature comfrey grows from a strong root system; plants will die back in the fall and emerge again from roots every spring.

FOXGLOVE *Digitalis purpurea*

Foxglove flowers are shaped like fingers of a glove. Foxglove is toxic and should not be used at home in any way that involves consuming. Magically, it is said to carry energy that pleases fairy folk, so plant it to enhance your communication with them.

How to Grow: Foxglove plants are prized for their bell-shaped flowers on tall stalks. It is typically grown throughout the temperate United States as biennials that last for two years. Foxglove grows in a range of light and soil conditions. Provide younger plants with consistent watering and increase water on hot days.

LADY'S MANTLE *Alchemilla vulgaris*

This plant is named for the scalloped leaf shape that is said to be reminiscent of the edges of a cloak; the lady referred to is the Virgin Mary. Magically, it is used to promote calm sleep and healing from the past, and can add extra energy to magic being done for or by women.

How to Grow: Lady's mantle is prized for both its beautiful foliage and its long-lasting yellow flowers. The perennial plant grows easily from seeds sown directly in the garden, transplants, or cuttings. Lady's mantle prefers bright locations and regular watering. In hotter climates, provide afternoon protection from direct sunlight.

MUGWORT *Artemisia vulgaris*

Mugwort is another ubiquitous witchy herb. A decoction of the leaves is said to help open your mind before you try divination. Magically, it is associated with prophetic dreams and divination, relaxation and tranquility, protection, banishing, and consecration.

How to Grow: Mugwort is popular with pollinators and prized for its distinctive smell. It is a vigorous plant that can reach up to 6 feet in height, with dark green stems that can look slightly purple. Mugwort likes full sun but can tolerate somewhat shadier conditions. Mugwort can be aggressive, so planting in containers is a good way to control it.

MULLEIN *Verbascum thapsus*

Medicinally, mullein soothes coughs, among many other uses. The hairlike fuzz on the leaves can irritate the mouth and throat, so strain it if you make a tea. Magically, mullein protects against danger and drives away negative energy.

How to Grow: Mullein is a plant that commonly grows in roadside ditches but does double duty as a garden plant. With a flower stalk that can reach up to 6 feet bearing yellow flowers on tall cones, mullein is a striking plant that tolerates full sun and dry soil. It also brings bees into your growing space.

VALERIAN *Valeriana officinalis*

Medicinally, valerian has sedative properties, and can also help relieve pain. Magically, it helps with self-confidence, finding the positive in a negative situation, and turning a negative situation to your benefit.

How to Grow: Valerian is a perennial herb that grows readily and easily in a wide range of conditions and spreads easily through wild-sown seeds. Mature valerian thrives in sunny conditions, growing into mature plants up to 5 feet tall and bearing white flowers. This plant is known for its cold tolerance. During the growing season, valerian prefers regular moisture.

VERVAIN *Verbena officinalis*

Vervain has varied magical applications. It can be used to cleanse, purify, and protect. It is a popular herb for enhancing psychic abilities and divinatory work. A pinch of vervain added to any charm or spell can increase the spell's chances of success. Medicinally, vervain can be used to reduce stress.

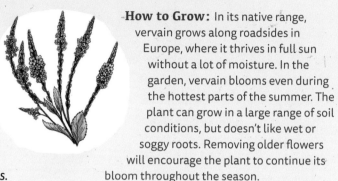

How to Grow: In its native range, vervain grows along roadsides in Europe, where it thrives in full sun without a lot of moisture. In the garden, vervain blooms even during the hottest parts of the summer. The plant can grow in a large range of soil conditions, but doesn't like wet or soggy roots. Removing older flowers will encourage the plant to continue its bloom throughout the season.

WORMWOOD *Artemisia absinthium*

Medicinally, wormwood is used as a tonic and stimulant. Extract of wormwood is used to make the liquor known as absinthe. Magical uses for wormwood include uncrossing or breaking a streak of bad luck, exorcism, banishing negative energy, enhancing psychic powers, and protection during travel.

How to Grow: Wormwood features beautiful silvery foliage and small yellow flowers on low, spreading plants that rarely get more than 3 feet tall. It prefers full sun but can tolerate some shade, and has high tolerance for drought and substandard soils.

YARROW *Achillea millefolium*

Yarrow is a common garden herb grown for its attractive silvery foliage. The leaves and stem of yarrow, harvested in late summer, have traditionally been used as a poultice to stanch bleeding. Magically, it is used for courage, healing, and love.

How to Grow: Depending on where you are, common yarrow is either a landscape plant with yellow flowers or a noxious weed that spreads without regard for other plants. A perennial, yarrow forms a small shrub about 3 feet tall and 3 feet wide. It does well in full sun and is tolerant of a wide range of soil conditions. Yarrow also can tolerate colder climates and, once established, is highly drought tolerant.

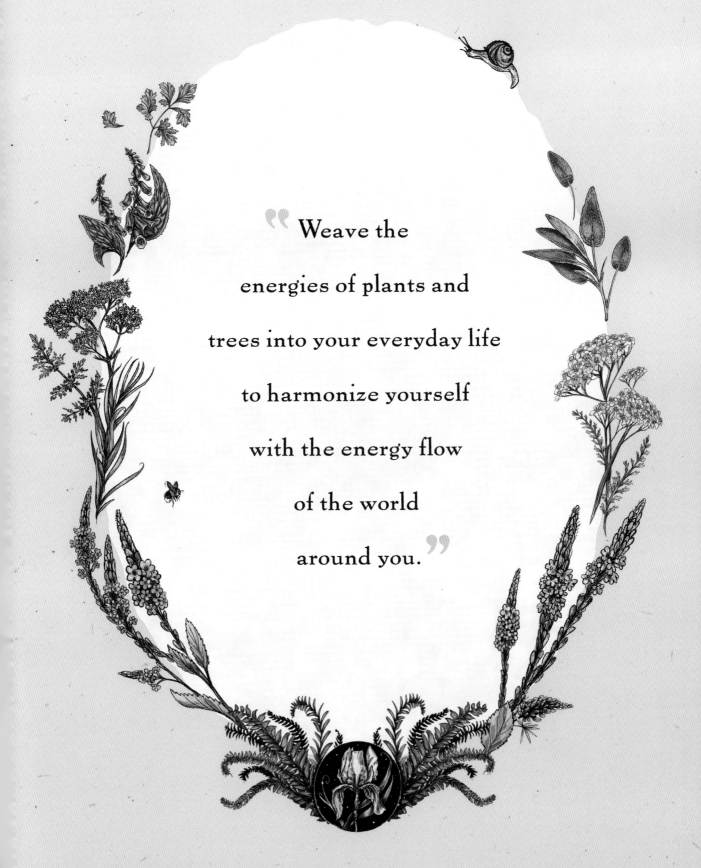

"Weave the energies of plants and trees into your everyday life to harmonize yourself with the energy flow of the world around you."

Clearing Simmer Pot

This is a good spell to do if your living space is feeling stale, or if the energy needs to be cleansed after a large gathering. It's also useful to do between seasons, around the time of a seasonal shift, to help stir lethargic energy. The suggested herbs carry general cleansing and purifying energies, and you can tweak them to reflect your intention or the time of year. For example, as winter winds down and spring begins to approach, you may want to include more energetic herbs, such as ginger, to help get things moving after the slow, quiet energy of winter.

YOU WILL NEED

Small saucepan or pot

Water (enough to fill pot halfway)

Fresh thyme sprig

Fresh rosemary sprig

Fresh sage sprig or leaves

3 whole cloves

Lemon slices (at least 3)

STEPS TO TAKE

1. Fill the pot about halfway with water. Set the pot on the stove.

2. Place the herbs, cloves, and lemon slices in the water.

3. Hold your hands above the pot and say:

   I call on the energies of thyme, rosemary, sage, clove,
   and lemon to cleanse this space. May unwanted energy
   be transformed into energy that is favorable to comfort,
   health, security, and life. May this space reflect my
   commitment to a spiritual path of positivity.
   I welcome the positive change.

4. Turn the heat to medium-low, or whatever your stove requires to get the water to a simmer. As the herbs and other ingredients warm, they will release an herbal scent and associated energies that will travel through your space.

5. Depending on how much water you put in the pot, the simmer can continue for a few hours. You can set a timer for however long you feel the spell needs to run and turn off the heat when you're finished. Don't let the water evaporate away completely.

6. Strain and compost the herbal matter after the water has cooled. You can dispose of the water, or use it to wipe down objects, doors, and window frames around the house in areas farthest from where the pot was simmering. This helps extend the spell's effect throughout your space.

Fruits

Fruit carries an energy based in fertility and abundance. All fruit carries seeds, which are the beginning of life. Whether we consume the seeds or not, their fertile energy permeates the whole fruit. Fruit is also a great way to consume seasonal energy. Here's a brief list of common fruits and their magical associations:

Blackberries
prosperity, protection, abundance

Blueberries
tranquility, peace, protection, prosperity

Banana
fertility, strength

Cherry
divination, love

Apple
health, longevity, love

Grape
prosperity, fertility

Orange
joy, health, purification

Lemon
purification, protection, health

Pear
health, prosperity, love

Peach
spirituality, fertility, love, harmony

Strawberries
love, peace, happiness, luck

Raspberries
strength, courage, healing

VEGETABLES

Like fruit, a vegetable is a visible seed container, and vegetables thus carry the magical associations of cycles and fertility. When you cook, therefore, you can also choose them for their magical associations. Here's a brief list of common vegetables and their magical associations:

Onion
protection, exorcism, healing, prosperity

Olives
healing, peace, lust, protection, potency, fertility

Beans
love, family, protection

Peas
love, abundance

Broccoli
protection, abundance

Tomato
protection, love

Carrots
fertility, health

Mushroom
strength, courage, healing, protection

Cucumber
fertility, healing, harmony

Lettuce
fertility, peace, harmony, protection

Corn
protection, divination, luck, fertility

Garlic
healing, protection, banishing, purification

MUSHROOMS and FUNGI

Mushrooms and fungi are often overlooked as part of a garden. You don't plant them the way you plant herbs or flowers, and they don't need the same kind of care. They're a fascinating thing to cultivate, however. Mushrooms are the most commonly recognized fungi. The cultivation of fungi is an interesting undertaking that offers you the chance to explore the energies connected to growing things that we don't often associate with a home garden.

Fungi are heavily associated with

organic recycling,

destruction,

and reconstruction.

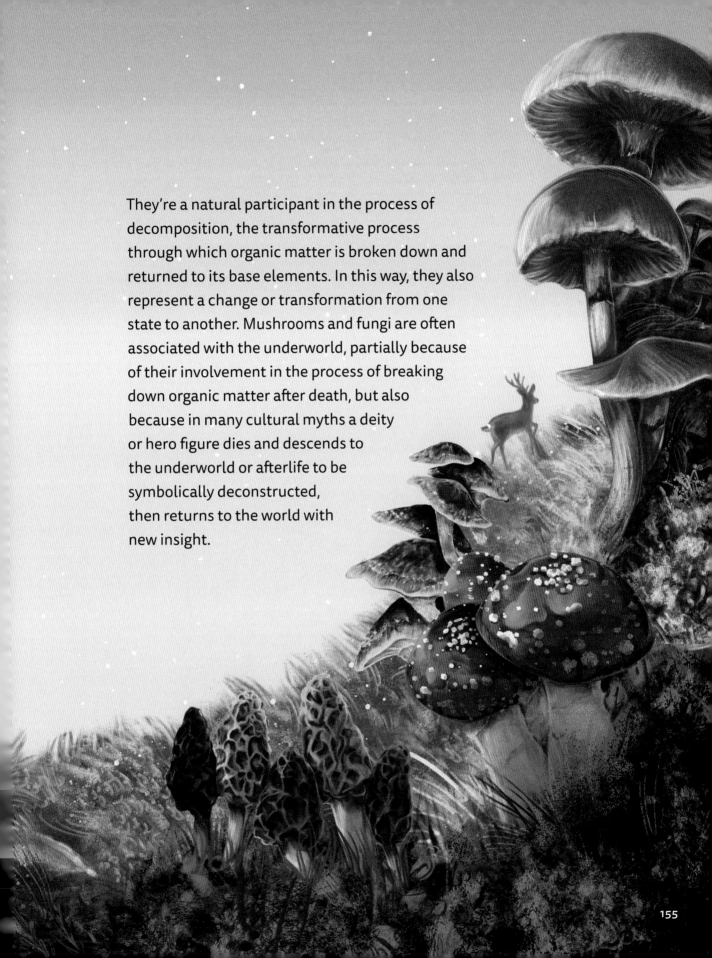

They're a natural participant in the process of decomposition, the transformative process through which organic matter is broken down and returned to its base elements. In this way, they also represent a change or transformation from one state to another. Mushrooms and fungi are often associated with the underworld, partially because of their involvement in the process of breaking down organic matter after death, but also because in many cultural myths a deity or hero figure dies and descends to the underworld or afterlife to be symbolically deconstructed, then returns to the world with new insight.

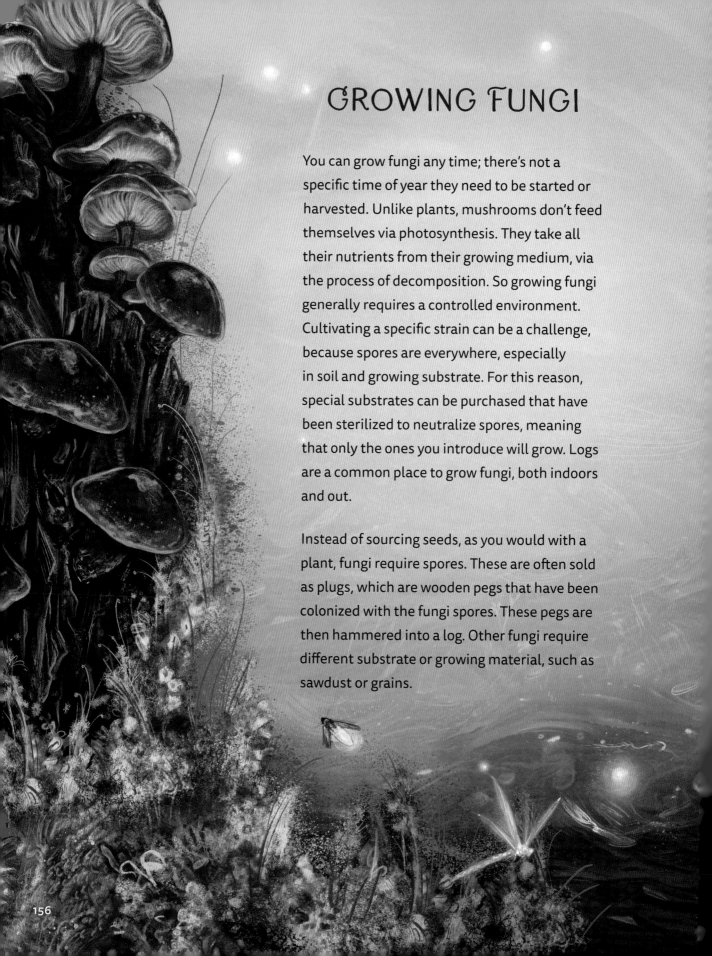

GROWING FUNGI

You can grow fungi any time; there's not a specific time of year they need to be started or harvested. Unlike plants, mushrooms don't feed themselves via photosynthesis. They take all their nutrients from their growing medium, via the process of decomposition. So growing fungi generally requires a controlled environment. Cultivating a specific strain can be a challenge, because spores are everywhere, especially in soil and growing substrate. For this reason, special substrates can be purchased that have been sterilized to neutralize spores, meaning that only the ones you introduce will grow. Logs are a common place to grow fungi, both indoors and out.

Instead of sourcing seeds, as you would with a plant, fungi require spores. These are often sold as plugs, which are wooden pegs that have been colonized with the fungi spores. These pegs are then hammered into a log. Other fungi require different substrate or growing material, such as sawdust or grains.

USING STONES:
THE BONES of the EARTH

Although they're not usually thought of as growing things like plants and trees, stones are sometimes referred to as "the bones of the earth." Small, nonperishable, and convenient, stones and crystals constitute a very useful element of the green witch's practice.

Stones have multiple uses
in green magic.

They can be empowered on their own and carried or left in specific areas. They can also be worn as jewelry, added to potpourris and herbal blends, powdered and added to incenses, added whole to incenses while they mature (but remove them before you burn the incense), added to oils, tucked into potted plants, and buried. The possibilities are endless.

Following are ten stones of use to the green witch.

Tree Agate

Tree agate is much like moss agate, except instead of looking like strands of green caught in translucent crystal, it looks like strands of green twining through an opaque white stone.

Carnelian

Carnelian is a milky orange stone. Magically, it is associated with success and manifestation.

Citrine

Citrine is yellow quartz and often appears as yellow ice or is yellow and white. It is found in points and as a tumbled stone. It works to calm nightmares, aids in digestion, focuses the mind, and enhances creativity.

Amethyst

Amethyst is purple quartz and is associated with psychic power, truth, balance, protection, and healing.

Malachite

A deep green stone with bands or circles of lighter green, malachite is associated with fertility and earth mysteries. Malachite is a wonderful stone for green witches to work with, for it helps strengthen your connection to the world of nature. Try carrying or wearing a piece of malachite while you communicate with the world of green. See how it affects your work and your perceptions.

Quartz (Clear)

A clear quartz crystal looks like ice, often with small inclusions (which do not affect the stone's energy at all). Quartz crystal amplifies energy, stores power, enhances psychic ability, and absorbs negativity. It can be found in tumbled form and in point form (which is how it grows) and is often set in jewelry. Quartz crystal is an excellent all-purpose stone to work with.

Quartz (Rose)

Another common stone, rose quartz looks like pink ice. Like other quartz crystals, rose quartz amplifies and stores energy. Rose quartz is specifically used to boost self-esteem and encourage self-love, for emotional healing, to foster affection, and to transform negative energy into positive, supportive energy.

Moonstone

A milky white stone, sometimes with overtones of green, peach, or gray, the moonstone is magically associated with protection during travel, children, love, and peace. It also has a connection to the Goddess.

Snowflake Obsidian

An opaque black stone with spots that look like white or pale gray snowflakes, this stone is used for protection. I prefer to use this form of obsidian in green witch work, as it reminds me of winter and midnight, two important parts of the natural cycle of days and seasons.

Tiger's Eye

A glossy, satiny, brown stone with bands of satiny dark gold, the tiger's eye is used for strength, courage, luck, and prosperity.

CLEANSING STONES

Before you use a stone, it is important to cleanse and purify it. Cleansing is a physical removal of dirt or debris; just wash the stone in plain water and scrub it with a cloth or brush if necessary. Purifying the stone means cleaning its energy. Before you use a stone for any magical purpose, it should always be purified. The hardness of the stone will dictate the best purification method; very soft stones should not be immersed in water, for example. There are several ways to purify a stone:

Leave it in sunlight or moonlight for a specific period of time.

Bury it in a small dish of salt for one to three days. Salt is a natural purifier. Never use salt to cleanse a stone that has iron in it, such as hematite, or if it is set in metal, for the metal will rust.

Bury it in a small dish of dirt for a measured period of time. Earth will accomplish the same purpose in the same way that salt does, though it may take longer.

Immerse the stone in water for a measured period of time. Moving water will purify it faster, although leaving the stone in a small bowl of water for a longer period will work as well.

ATTUNING TO STONES

Before you use a stone for a magical purpose, get to know its particular energy so that when you test its energy later on, you have an idea of how much purification it requires. When you first bring a stone home, cleanse and purify it using one of the previous methods for one full week to ensure that it has been completely cleared of any foreign energy.

When the week is up, it is time to attune yourself to the stone.

1   *Begin by finding a quiet space and settling down with the stone and your green witch notebook.*

2   *Take three deep breaths, releasing tension and focusing on the stone in your hand with each exhalation.*

3   *Begin by testing the energy of the stone. How does the stone's energy feel to you? Make as many observations and associations as you can. Remember to write them down. What is important is that you are making personal observations about the energy.*

Once you have an idea of how the energy of the stone feels to you while it is completely natural and unaffected by any other energy, you will be able to evaluate the stone before any future use to determine how much purification it will need.

Empowering Stones

To prepare a stone for magical use once it has been purified, you must program or empower it. This step aligns the stone's natural energy with your magical intention. While the stone's natural energies will function even if you do not empower it with your magical intention, they will function in accordance to your desire much more efficiently if you program it with your precise need and magical goal.

1. To program a stone with your intention, hold it between your palms. Close your eyes and take three deep breaths, centering yourself and focusing on your magical goal.
2. Visualize your goal as already achieved, which means you should take a minute or two to daydream about how terrific you'll feel once the situation is the way you want it.
3. Now visualize a sparkling light forming around your hands. This sparkling light is the energy summoned from within you to empower the stone. It is energy programmed with your magical goal. Imagine the sparkling light being absorbed into the stone.

4. At this point, say aloud what your goal is and what the stone is to be used for. For example, if you are programming it for financial success or abundance, you may say:

This stone brings me prosperity.

Some people find it easier to repeat a phrase like this over and over in order to raise and focus the energy upon what they are empowering. I tend to be a very quiet green witch, so I quietly whisper my chosen phrase over and over until the words become a stream of sound. I visualize that sound being directed into the stone.

5. Once the energy has been absorbed into the stone, the stone has been programmed with your magical intention and empowered for that use.

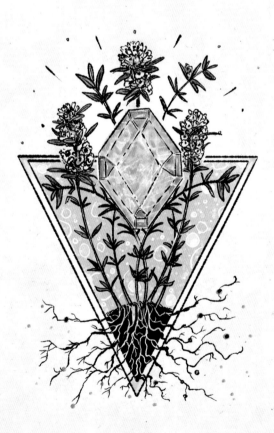

CHAPTER 6

Keep a GREEN WITCH Garden

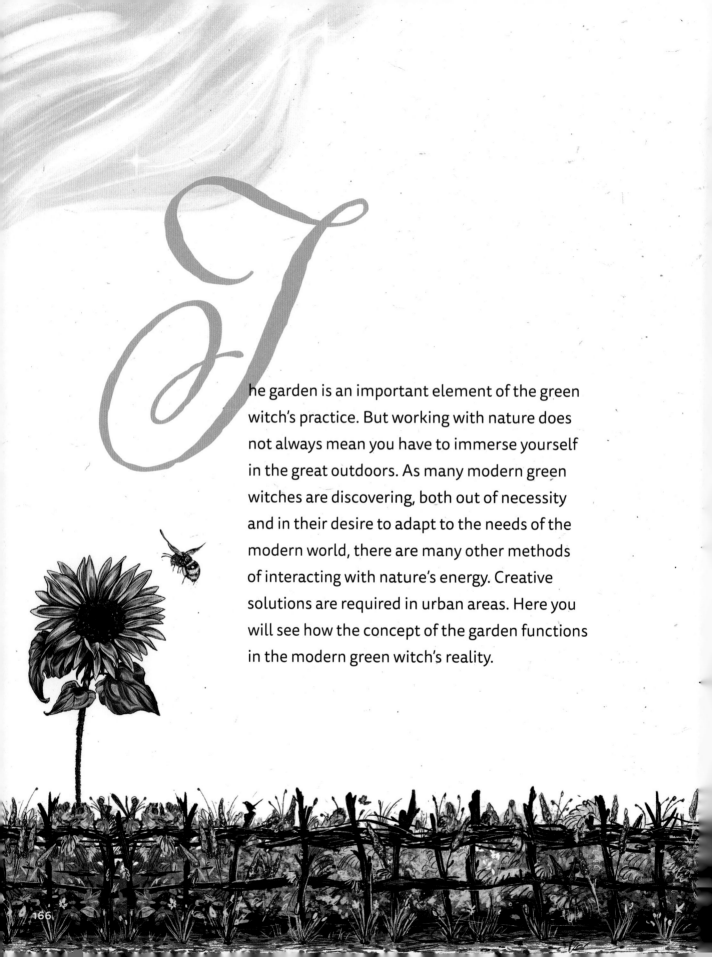

The garden is an important element of the green witch's practice. But working with nature does not always mean you have to immerse yourself in the great outdoors. As many modern green witches are discovering, both out of necessity and in their desire to adapt to the needs of the modern world, there are many other methods of interacting with nature's energy. Creative solutions are required in urban areas. Here you will see how the concept of the garden functions in the modern green witch's reality.

The POWER in a GARDEN

The practice of green witchcraft is innately tied to the agricultural cycle, which dictated the rhythm of the lives of our ancestors. The agricultural societies of yesteryear focused on the seasonal changes of soil and crops. Witchcraft's concern with fertility, sowing, tending, and reaping (metaphorically and otherwise) is rooted in that agricultural tradition. It thus makes a certain kind of sense that the green witch has a strong spiritual and personal connection to nature and the land. The connection to nature is also a practical one. The witch's garden provides a ready source of food as well as components of spells and ingredients for various remedies. Working with a garden of any kind also allows you to meditate on the concept of harmony and balance in a completely different way. There is a very real give-and-take of energy involved in tending a garden. The time and care you put into maintaining the garden is directly reflected in the garden's health and what you harvest.

Garden Protection Spell

If your garden is indoors, take soil from each plant, or from roughly the four corners of the space they're in. Use a protection oil blend you've created, or a single oil you associate with protection, such as clove, lemon, rosemary, eucalyptus, or pepper. Decide a few things before you perform this spell. Where will you put your protection packet? Are you going to bury or hang it in your garden? Are you going to keep it inside, tucked in a small bowl or cup of earth? You'll also need to decide on a symbol you associate with protection for the talisman.

This spell should be done annually. If the talisman wasn't buried, you can declare its work complete and decommission it, thanking it for its work. Disassemble the packet, burn the paper and thread, cleanse the stones in your chosen method, and start again with a new sketch or printout.

YOU WILL NEED

Small blue, white, or green candle in a candleholder (not a tea light)

Matches or a lighter

Overhead sketch of garden, or a photo of your garden on regular paper

Pinch of soil from the four corners of your garden or property

Protection oil

Small piece of obsidian

Small piece of malachite, moss agate, or tree agate

Small feather or toothpick

Blue or white thread or cotton/wool yarn (not acrylic or polyester)

STEPS TO TAKE

1. Cleanse the supplies and declare them free of unsupportive energy. Do this with incense or simply by holding your hands over the materials. Say: *I banish unsupportive energy from these supplies. I welcome positive and protective energies to remain and lend themselves to this protection.*

2. Light your candle and declare sacred space in your preferred way.

3. Lay your sketch/photo out on your workspace. Add the pinches of soil on the paper; declare this your garden by law of contagion and similarity: *I name this my garden. What happens here happens to the associated space.*

4. Dot protection oil on the four corners of the paper.

5. Speak your intention of protection into the two stones: *I invoke the protective energies of this stone. May it extend its defense to my garden, and safeguard it from harm.*

6. Lay the stones in the center of the paper.

7. Fold the corners over to meet in the middle, then the resulting angles. At each fold, speak your intention into the talisman: *I wrap these stones in the representation of my garden, making them one.*

8. Fold until it's a very small packet.

9. Draw your symbol on the packet with oil, using the feather or toothpick.

10. Tie the packet shut with the thread, wrapping and tying several times (at least three). Speak your sealed intent into it: *I name you protection, I name you guardian, I name you complete.*

11. With the candle, carefully drip wax on the knots and where the edges of the paper meet. Pinch out the candle with thanks and keep it; you can burn it regularly to send fresh energy to the talisman packet, or keep it until the time comes to make a new packet.

12. Either take the packet into garden to bury or keep inside in a chosen location to work its magic.

DESIGN YOUR GARDEN

The modern green witch faces several challenges when it comes to gardening and creating a personal space in which to commune with nature. In a city or suburb, many people do not have an ideal space in which to lay out a garden. If you don't have a strip of earth somewhere along the path to your front door, or if you're bound to an apartment and have no land at all, you may be surprised to find out that you, in fact, have several options. Check with your city hall or environmental division to see if your city sponsors public garden space. You can apply for one of these garden plots, which are usually fenced off and protected, often for free or at a low rental cost. You may have to travel to it, but you can grow whatever you like within legal parameters. Or, if you prefer something closer to home, you can create a balcony or window garden.

Here are questions to answer before you start planting your garden:

What will be the purpose of your garden? Do you intend to grow herbs to cook with or to make tea with? Vegetables to eat? Fruit to bake with? Is your garden to be a peaceful retreat, your personal connection to nature, your power place? If you plan well enough, you can create a sacred space where you will carry on your personal green witch dialogue with nature. Watering, weeding, and caring for a window box can be just as rewarding as sitting in the middle of a national park.

How much time will you devote to maintaining your garden?

What is your budget?

When will you be using your space? Will you be gardening or enjoying your space in the daytime or in the evening? Because some plants bloom and release their scent after dark, your plant selection can reflect your schedule.

Do you want your garden to reflect the style of the rest of your home? Or do you want to do something dramatically different to contrast with your usual style?

Answering these questions will help you determine what kind of garden to develop.

Invocation of Growing Success

This meditation can be done in the winter when you are planning your garden, in the later spring when you plant, or whenever you design a new garden. With some tweaks, I also use it when I plant a new acquisition or welcome a new houseplant. It's versatile, so use it whenever you feel it's appropriate.

Spirits of Nature, of my garden and home,
Guide me in my work.

May I make good choices for the needs of myself, my family,
And the land and its denizens.

May I listen to the local energies and respond to them appropriately.

May I research well to understand what is invasive, and what
My geographic area needs to support its local wildlife.

Bless me, this space, and the plants
With success, health, and long, productive lives.

STARTING SEEDLINGS

While sprouting plants from seed to repot outdoors in a container garden is a wonderful way to forge a connection with your garden from the very first stirrings of life, it is often a challenge. Try it. If nothing sprouts, don't despair. There's no shame in buying hardened seedlings from a nursery or garden center and planting those in your containers.

Be sure to use good potting soil. To ease drainage, blend another medium with it, such as peat moss. Regular garden soil isn't right for container gardens. They need soil rich in nutrients because there's so little soil in the container. If garden soil is the only thing available to you, then blend equal parts of sand and peat moss into it. Ask your garden center about fertilizers for container gardens to maintain a high level of nutrients for your plants.

Perform regular maintenance. Regular general maintenance is the key to keeping your garden in balance. Look at your plants every day. Look for yellowed leaves, limp foliage, dead flowers. Nip off dying areas and water dry plants. Clay pots are porous and will lose water faster than glazed or plastic containers. Rotate pots so that all sides of the plant get equal light. Being sensitive to the status of your garden will allow you to pick up on small oddities before they grow into problems.

Water consistently. Your watering schedule will depend on your weather, the size of your containers, and what kind of plants you're growing. Containers tend to not hold a lot of water, because there isn't a lot of earth in them. The water dries up or is rapidly absorbed by the plant. A good rule is to water every couple of days unless you're in a dry spell, in which case water every day. If carrying heavy cans or pitchers of water is difficult for you, consider getting a hose attachment for your kitchen tap.

CARE for YOUR GARDEN NATURALLY

There are several ways to cultivate your garden naturally. After all, the idea of using chemical ingredients on your garden to cultivate growth or kill invading insects is contrary to the green witch way. Here are tips for using two natural methods to increase the bounty of your garden: composting and ecologically-friendly pest management. Working with a garden is a continuous lesson in patience, acceptance, and recognition that nature functions as an independent system.

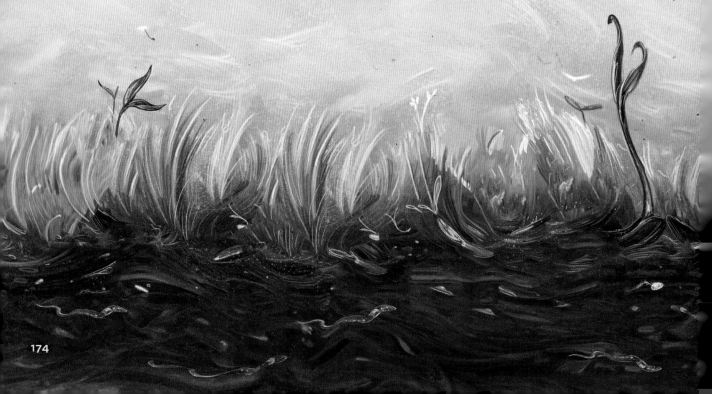

COMPOSTING

Composting is the practice of returning organic matter to the earth where it can decompose and add its nutrients to the soil. Although composting is usually thought of as something landowners do, urban dwellers can also compost easily in a modified fashion. Vermicomposting, or using red worms to break down organic matter, is one option. Vermicomposting kits can be ordered online or obtained from ecological shops or garden centers. A less expensive and easier alternative is a compost bin. You can place the bin outdoors, which most apartment dwellers prefer, but if you have no balcony, you can put it in a dark corner of the kitchen or laundry room. Whatever the location, compost requires three things:

Warmth ❧ Dark ❧ Food

The warmth is achieved by placing your bin close to the wall if on the balcony or storing it under your sink if indoors. The dark is obtained by using an opaque material for the bin and by having a tight-fitting lid. The food comes from finely chopped vegetable and fruit scraps. Never add meat products or anything with grease to your compost bin. These will decompose, all right, but it will smell dreadful, unbalance the compost you're building, and attract pests. You can add:

Tea leaves

Vegetable scraps

Eggshells

Dead garden matter

Fruit scraps

Coffee grounds

Every time you add scraps, give the compost a stir. Once in a while, do a complete turn over with a small shovel or trowel to aerate the soil.

The ideal container for composting is a plastic garbage can or a large plastic bin. Line the bottom with dead leaves or shredded newspaper. Put a layer of earth on top of that, then add your first batch of chopped food scraps and a bit of water. Stir it with a stick and replace the lid. The lid holds the humidity inside as the food decomposes, but it's a good idea to "water" your compost to keep it damp (but not wet). Add a bit more dry material, such as more shredded newspaper or earth, each week to ensure a balance of carbon and nitrogen. In about three months, your compost will be ready for use.

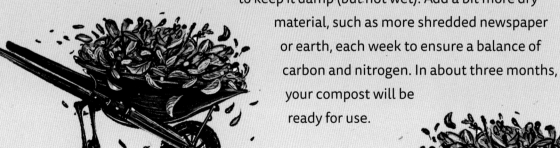

Compost Infusion

A compost infusion is made by filtering water through the compost. This produces a nutrient-rich liquid that you can use to help nourish and protect your plants both above ground and below. Use it to water your houseplants and garden plants and to spray the foliage to battle pests, illness, and pollution damage. To make a simple compost infusion:

1. Loosely fill a bucket a third to halfway full of compost. Give the compost a couple of turns with the trowel to aerate it properly and break up any clumps.
2. Pour warm water (not hot or boiling) over the compost and allow it to sit for two to three days.
3. Carefully decant the resulting brown water into another bucket or pitcher.
4. Allow the wet compost to dry out to its usual damp state before returning it to your compost bin.

PEST MANAGEMENT

If you're working with a container garden, you'll most likely
have to deal with insects and other pests. Here are green witch–friendly
things you can use to help protect your plants:

Natural Insecticide

Make an extract of garlic, onion, or
hot pepper. Take 3 tablespoons of the
vegetable matter and chop it finely
or purée it in a blender with a bit of
water. Add 2 cups of water and steep
it overnight or for a full day. Strain
it, dilute it so that the total amount
of liquid equals 1 liter or 1 quart, and
pour it into a spray bottle. Test it on
a leaf of the affected plant; if the leaf
responds poorly, dilute the spray
more and test again.

Bleach Solution

To eliminate stubborn pests, you can
use a solution of one part bleach to
forty parts water. Spray this over the
foliage and stem of the plant, but do
not soak the earth. Rinse well with
clear water. This is easier if you place
a plastic bag or some such thing over
the earth and the container or tilt the
container so that the runoff doesn't
land in the pot.

When you spray, no matter what you spray with, remember to practice safe spraying habits:

Wear protection.
Always wear gloves, long sleeves, and a mask when spraying with insecticides, even natural ones.

Wait for a calm day.
Don't spray when there is a strong breeze.

Do not spray during the heat of the day.
Do it first thing in the morning or wait until the evening.

Test first.
Always perform a test on a small area of each type of plant before you spray them all. This way you can test the strength of the spray as well as the plant's reaction to it.

Never spray all your plants indiscriminately.
These sprays are not all-purpose preventives. They are meant to target a specific problem. They can also kill off the beneficial insects and microbes that live among your plants.

FILL YOUR HOME with HOUSEPLANTS

If growing plants outdoors is impossible in your situation, or if you want green indoors as well as out, try houseplants.

When you bring home a new houseplant, make sure to do a gentle energy purification to help acclimatize it to the energy of your living space. This also removes any negativity that may be clinging to it. You can never remove the basic energy of an object, so don't worry about removing the positive energy associated with the plant. To do an energy purification:

1.

Run your hand over the plant about 1–2 inches away from the foliage.

2.

Visualize scooping up any black or smoky energy around the plant.

3.

Flick your hand as if you were shaking water off it to remove and disperse the negative energy.

Spell

Houseplant Blessing

Choosing what sorts of houseplants to bring into your home is as important as choosing the plants you grow outdoors. Think about the light that fills your living space, the direction from which it comes, and how bright it is. Think about how dry or humid your living space is and the general temperatures. Finally, it is important to remember that like all plants, houseplants absorb negative energy. However, because they are potted in a small amount of earth, they cannot transform the energy with the same success that outdoor plants in the ground can. Be kind to your houseplants: give them an appropriate fertilizer, repot them before it becomes necessary, and purify them regularly. Give a plant a good start by welcoming it into your home:

1. Bless a pitcher of clean, fresh water by saying the following:

   Spirits of Earth, Water, Fire, and Air,
   I ask your blessing on this water.
   Endow it with strength, protection, and peace,
   And may the plants that drink of it be similarly blessed.

2. Give your new houseplant as much of this sacred drink as it requires. Use the rest for your current houseplants.

CHAPTER 7

CREATE *and* CRAFT GREEN WITCH MAGIC

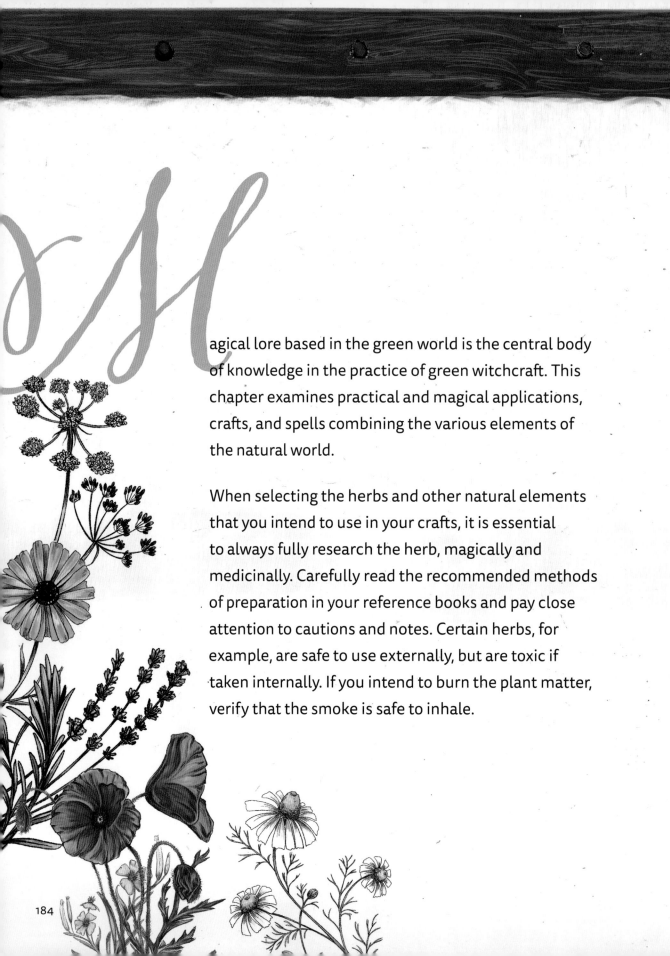

Magical lore based in the green world is the central body of knowledge in the practice of green witchcraft. This chapter examines practical and magical applications, crafts, and spells combining the various elements of the natural world.

When selecting the herbs and other natural elements that you intend to use in your crafts, it is essential to always fully research the herb, magically and medicinally. Carefully read the recommended methods of preparation in your reference books and pay close attention to cautions and notes. Certain herbs, for example, are safe to use externally, but are toxic if taken internally. If you intend to burn the plant matter, verify that the smoke is safe to inhale.

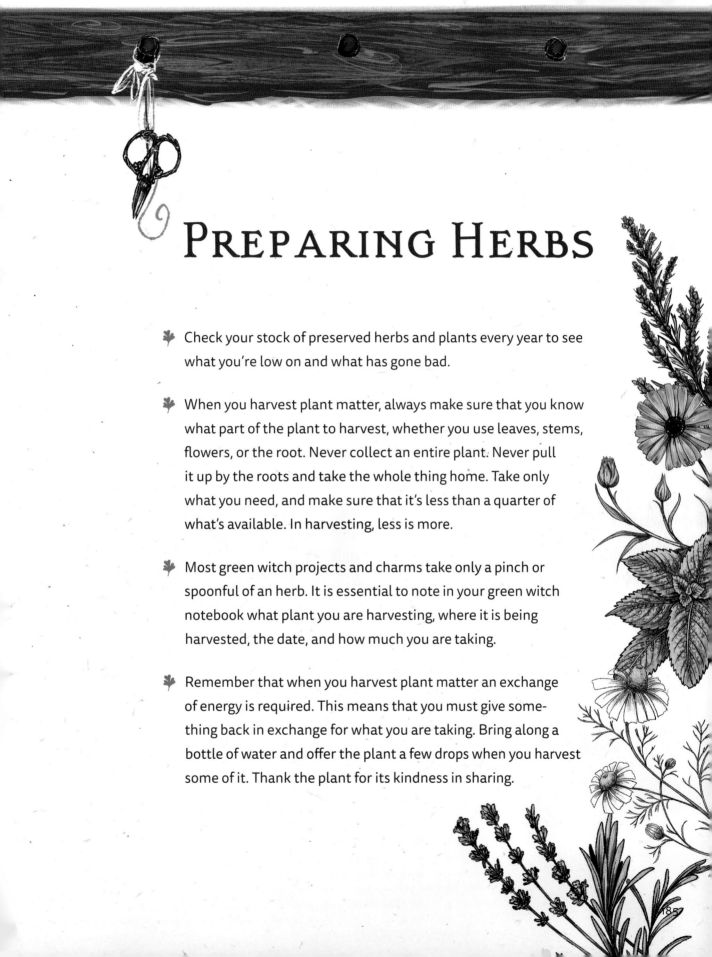

PREPARING HERBS

🌿 Check your stock of preserved herbs and plants every year to see what you're low on and what has gone bad.

🌿 When you harvest plant matter, always make sure that you know what part of the plant to harvest, whether you use leaves, stems, flowers, or the root. Never collect an entire plant. Never pull it up by the roots and take the whole thing home. Take only what you need, and make sure that it's less than a quarter of what's available. In harvesting, less is more.

🌿 Most green witch projects and charms take only a pinch or spoonful of an herb. It is essential to note in your green witch notebook what plant you are harvesting, where it is being harvested, the date, and how much you are taking.

🌿 Remember that when you harvest plant matter an exchange of energy is required. This means that you must give something back in exchange for what you are taking. Bring along a bottle of water and offer the plant a few drops when you harvest some of it. Thank the plant for its kindness in sharing.

DRYING HERBS

If you're not using the plant matter fresh, then it must be dried before you store it. Before drying, shake, brush, or wash off any dirt. To air-dry it, lay the leaves or flowers out on an old screen or on cheesecloth and allow it to dry in a well-ventilated area. You can also bundle the stems together with an elastic band or string and hang the bunch indoors in a dry place with good air circulation, out of direct sunlight. Don't leave a bundle of herbs hanging for too long, or it will become dusty. To protect it from dust, or if the stem plant has seeds or fragile bits that may fall off as it dries, slip it in a paper bag and secure the bag around the stems with string before hanging it to dry. To prepare a plant for storage, strip the leaves off the stems over a sheet of newspaper or a clean cloth.

FREEZING HERBS

If you wish to use herbs like rosemary or peppermint fresh at a later date, you can pick them and store them in the freezer. For short-term storage, you can simply tumble sturdy leaves into a small paper bag, fold it over, and store it in the freezer door. Be sure to write the herb, the date, and where it was harvested on the bag. To keep herbs longer, rinse them under cold water, blot them dry with a paper towel, chop them roughly, and spread them on a baking sheet. Put the baking sheet in the freezer until the herbs have frozen, then store them in zip-top freezer bags. Mark the bag clearly with the name of the herb, the date, and where you harvested it. To use, simply open the bag and take out what you need. If leaves or flowers have frozen together, take the mass out and chop off what you need with a knife.

EXTRACTING the ENERGIES of HERBS

Herbs and plant matter are most commonly prepared for use in an infusion, which you may better know as tea. Teas aren't used only for consumption, of course, which is why books on magical and spiritual applications use the word "infusion." In this book, if I use the word "tea" I'm referring to something you'll drink; if I use the word "infusion" I'm talking about a liquid that you'll use in some other application.

The basic preparation is known as a "simple," which is a single-herb preparation. This is the best and easiest way to access the energy of an individual plant and the safest way to test new herbs for their effects.

The following four methods explain how to extract and preserve the energies and benefits of various herbs:

1.

Infusion is the process by which leaves and/or flowers are steeped for a period of time in water of a particular temperature. As the water cools, the herbal matter steeps. This technique allows the water to extract the benefits and energies from fragile herbal matter. An infusion creates the weakest extraction.

2.

Maceration is the process by which herbal matter is steeped in a solvent such as vinegar, alcohol, or glycerin. The result is called a tincture. Tinctures are commonly used for medicinal purposes, usually by adding a few drops to a glass of water or spoonful of honey and consuming it. Tinctures can also be used magically.

3.

Decoction is the process by which denser herbal matter (such as roots, twigs, or bark) is boiled in water for a specific period of time. A decoction creates a slightly stronger extraction than infusion.

4.

Enfleurage is the method by which oils and energies are extracted from herbal matter by soaking the herb in an oil or a fat, either heated or at room temperature. The result is an essential oil if the liquid is at room temperature, and a pomade if the result is a solid. Your oil will vary in strength depending on how long you saturate your herbal matter and how frequently you change the depleted herbal matter for fresh herbal matter.

In both medicine and magic, there are a variety of ways to apply herbal energies.

The four methods previously described result in liquids of varying viscosity. To deliver those liquids in methods other than pouring or drinking them, they can be combined with another base to offer a more flexible application. The results of mixing these liquids with another base include the following possibilities:

1.

Salves are created by melting beeswax and adding a liquid extract (usually an oil) to it, then allowing it to cool. Infusions and decoctions aren't used in preparing a salve because they aren't strong enough to carry the required energy or extract. Salves are rubbed into the body or an object.

2.

Soaps take your liquid extracts and combine them with a base of fats designed to raise dirt from a surface, enabling it to be washed away. Magical soaps are particularly interesting because they also pull negative or undesirable energy from an object and allow it to be washed away.

3.

Liniments are liquids that are usually alcohol based. A liniment is designed to be rubbed briskly on the body.

BLESSING YOUR CREATIONS

Although everything has an innate energy and you empower every preparation or craft object you create with your intention, sometimes it's nice to seal or enhance the combined energies. Performing the elemental blessing on the following pages upon an object can help dedicate it to the purpose you intend it for. It also sends a signal to your own psyche that your work is finished and is now performing the function for which it was designed.

Elemental Blessing

This blessing can be performed as the final step of any project or upon new objects or items intended for a shrine. In essence, this act purifies the object and then blesses it with positive energy. Blessing gives the object the best possible start. It calls in positive energy and specific intentions.

The blessing is written with the assumption that the object you will bless is small enough to be held in your hands. If it is not, place it on or next to your workspace and adjust your actions accordingly. If you have previously cleansed the object you intend to bless, or if you have empowered it, you may skip steps 2 through 6.

Instead of a stick of incense in a holder you can use herbal incense and a self-lighting charcoal briquette in a heatproof dish.

YOU WILL NEED

Small dish of salt or earth (or a small crystal or other stone)

Stick of incense in a holder

Candle in candleholder

Small dish of water

Matches or a lighter

Object to be blessed

STEPS TO TAKE

1. Arrange each elemental symbol on your workspace, either in a square or in a line. Light the incense and the candle. Take three deep breaths to release stress so you can focus on your task.

2. Pick up the object with one hand or lay it on your workspace in front of you. With your other hand, take a pinch of the salt or earth and sprinkle it gently over the object (or take the crystal or stone in your hand and touch it to the object), saying: *By earth I cleanse you.*

3. Pick up the candle and pass it around the object in a counterclockwise direction, saying: *By fire I cleanse you.*

4. Pick up the incense and pass it counterclockwise around the object, saying: *By air I cleanse you.*

5. Touch your fingertips to the water and sprinkle it over the object, saying: *By water I cleanse you.*

6. Close your eyes, take three slow breaths, and focus on the object.

7. Take another pinch of earth or salt and sprinkle it over the object (or touch the crystal or stone to it), saying: *You are blessed by earth.*

8. Pass the object carefully over the candle flame, making sure not to burn yourself or the object, saying: *You are blessed by fire.*

9. Pass the object through the smoke of the incense, saying: *You are blessed by air.*

10. Touch your fingertips to the water and sprinkle it on the object, saying: *You are blessed by water.*

11. Hold the object up in the air, or if it is too heavy place your hands upon it where it lies, and say: *I ask the Green Spirit of the Universe to bless this object in the name of Earth and of all Nature.*

Herbal Incense

If you use incense in stick form, then you are familiar with the sweet and gentle smoke created by lighting one end of the stick, gently blowing out the flame, and resting the stick in a censer or incense boat to smolder slowly.

Herbal incense is a completely different experience. It is a wonderful method of experimenting with the bounty of nature.

When you create your own herbal incense, you can mix and match the kinds of magical energies you wish to weave together, tailoring them precisely to your specific goal. You can make as much or as little as you like, empowering the blend with your own personal energy.

Herbal incense must always be made with dried herbs. Fresh herbs will not burn correctly and will rot if you attempt to store them in a container. If the only sample of the herb you wish to use in your blend is fresh, you can dry them with one of two methods:

1.

Spread the herb on a baking sheet and place it in a barely warm oven (100°F) with the door slightly open for 45 minutes to 1 hour, watching it carefully.

2.

Spread the herb in a single layer on a paper towel and microwave it for 30 seconds on high. Check to see how dry it is. You can microwave in 10-second increments for further drying.

Some green witches, concerned that the microwave damages the herb's energy, recoil at the idea of microwaving their herbs, whereas other green witches have no qualms about using modern equipment such as a microwave, a juicer, or an electric coffee grinder to prepare their magical supplies. It's your choice. As a modern green witch, use what you have at your disposal, as long as you feel comfortable with it.

TEST YOUR HERBS

Before you blend herbal incense, it's important to do some research to find out what kinds of herbs and flowers are best for your recipe.* Once you have a short list of the herbs you'd like to use in your magical incense, take an hour or so to light a single charcoal briquette and drop a tiny pinch of each herb by itself onto the ignited surface. Burning herbal matter will not smell like the fresh herb. In fact, it usually smells like some sort of variation on burning leaves or grass clippings. Testing each herb alone will give you an idea of what it smells like. As it burns, make notes in your green witch journal about:

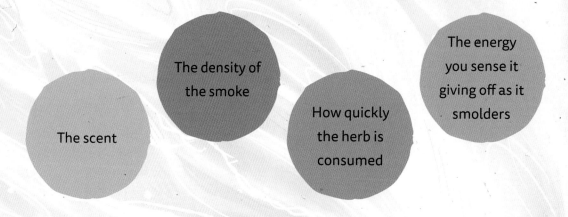

The scent

The density of the smoke

How quickly the herb is consumed

The energy you sense it giving off as it smolders

*Before you burn any herb, it is important to look up its toxicity. If it's poisonous to touch or eat, chances are the smoke is also poisonous to breathe.

It is also important to make a note of how you react physically to the herb. It is better to discover now in a test run that you react badly to a certain herb than when you're attempting to use it magically. Once you've tested each herb, you're ready to work with proportions. Do you want to add more of one herb and perhaps only a pinch of another? Much of the green witch's work is intuitive, which means that you'll feel drawn to something without necessarily having solid information or reasoning to support your feeling.

TEST YOUR RESINS

One of the plain truths about using herbal incense is that it doesn't always smell as sweet as store-bought stick incense. Adding resin in an equal amount to your herbal blend will not only improve the incense's burn rate but will also provide a more agreeable base note to your burning incense. Before adding one or more resins to an herbal blend, however, drop a single grain of the resin or a tiny pinch of powder onto a charcoal briquette to acquaint yourself with the scent of the resin on its own. As it burns, make notes in your green witch journal about:

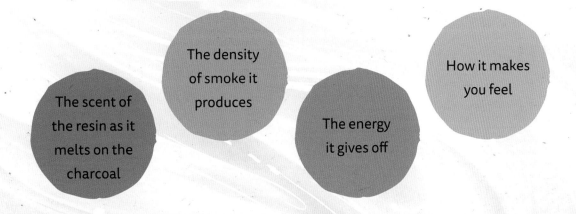

The scent of the resin as it melts on the charcoal

The density of smoke it produces

The energy it gives off

How it makes you feel

Resins are usually sold by weight in packets of rough grains or chips. Generally, it is best to powder your resin before blending it with your herbal matter. This will entail a bit of grinding on your part with a stone mortar and pestle (wood is unsuitable for grinding resins) or using a small coffee grinder reserved only for grinding herbs and resins. The powdered resin will blend better with the dried herbs and yield a smoother burn. Try using one or more of the resins on the following pages as a base for your herbal incense (remember that the amount of resin should equal the total amount of herbal matter).

Copal

This resin comes in various shades of white, gold, and black, and the scent is slightly different for each kind. Golden copal is most common. Copal is the petrified sap of the *Bursera odorata* and has an appealing sweet scent that makes an excellent base for floral or lighter herbal incense blends. Copal carries an energy that is particularly good for love, house blessings, dedications, meditation, protection, celebration, solar energy, and creating sacred space.

Frankincense

One of the most popular resins, the golden-toned frankincense is the solidified sap of the *Boswellia carterii* tree, sometimes called the olibanum. It has a slightly spicy-sweet scent and makes an excellent all-purpose base for just about any herbal incense. Frankincense is traditionally associated with sanctity, purification, meditation, protection, joy, celebration, solar energy, and consecration.

Myrrh

Another common resin, myrrh is brownish and has a darker, slightly bittersweet scent. It comes from the *Commiphora myrrha*, or gum myrrh tree, and carries the magical associations of sanctity, honoring the dead and the spirit world, purification, and healing. Myrrh adds a bit of extra power to any herbal incense; adding just a grain or two will do the job.

Sandalwood

Often blended into herbal incenses or used as a base, sandalwood isn't technically a resin, but a powdered or shredded wood. Available both in red (*Adenanthera pavonina*) and white (*Santalum album*), sandalwood is generally associated with spirituality, purification, meditation, peace, healing, and protection.

Dragon's Blood

Benzoin

Styrax

This red resin is the petrified sap of the palm tree known as *Daemonorops draco*, or the dragon's blood palm. It is one of the key ingredients in violin stain. It is sticky and will cling to your fingers and tools. Dragon's blood is frequently used for protection, purification, and as a general addition to your spells as an all-purpose power boost.

This grayish resin is usually found in powdered form. It comes from the *Styrax benzoin* tree and has a light, clean, slightly sweet scent. It is excellent for purifying, healing, prosperity, and attraction in general.

Sometimes spelled storax, this black resin is a softer, earthier resin than those previously listed. It comes from the *Liquidambar styraciflua* tree. It is excellent for healing and grounding.

Resins have been used for centuries in various cultures as sweet-smelling offerings to the gods. They carry various magical associations just as herbs do.

BLENDING HERBAL INCENSE

When you create a recipe for herbal incense, select a combination of herbs and resins that will support your goal with their energies. For example, a prosperity incense may include one part benzoin as the resin base, with one part herbal blend of mint, basil, and cinnamon, all of which are associated with prosperity. Like other witches, green witches often like to work in multiples of three on top of their base ingredient. Three is a number associated with the Goddess. You may also like to work with a multiple of four to honor the four elements. There are no firm rules; use what you feel drawn to using. But remember that more is not necessarily better. The basic steps to blending herbal incense are simple:

1. If necessary, gently grind the resin until the pieces are in small granules. Be careful not to overgrind them, or the heat produced by the mortar and pestle or coffee grinder will make the resin sticky.
2. Crumble or powder the dried herbs and place them in the jar with the resin. Cap it and shake until the ingredients are well blended.
3. Write down the final recipe in your journal, along with the magical purpose and the date on which you blended it, and label the container.

To further enhance your herbal incense, add up to three drops of essential oil to the mixture before you cap and shake it. Again, consider your magical goal and choose an appropriate essential oil. Do not use more than three drops, or the incense will be too wet to burn. Once your herbal incense is blended, you may use it right away or leave it to sit and allow the energies to blend for a week or so before using it.

Empower Your Herbal Incense

You can use your incense as it is. However, like any other magical craft or preparation, empowering the incense will weave the energies together better and focus them specifically upon your magical goal. There are two ways to empower your herbal incense. Most green witches employ them both. The first is to visualize your magical goal as you grind and blend each herb and resin. This method allows you to program each component separately. The second method is as follows:

1. Hold the jar of finished incense in your hands. Take three deep breaths to focus. Think of your magical goal.

2. Visualize a sparkling light forming around the jar in your hands. This sparkling light is the energy that empowers the incense, the energy associated with your magical goal.

3. Imagine the sparkling light being absorbed into the blend of resins and herbs. The herbal incense has now been energized with your magical goal. It is empowered for that use.

BURNING HERBAL INCENSE

Herbal incense is burned on small, round charcoal briquettes that are available at New Age and religious supply shops. To burn herbal incense, you will need the following things:

1.

A small, round briquette of self-igniting charcoal*

2.

A heatproof censer with a layer of sand or earth in it

3.

A lighter or long-stemmed matches

Self-igniting charcoal briquettes come in various sizes. I don't recommend the ½-inch size, as they are easy to smother with a spoonful of incense and prone to falling apart or exploding if not handled correctly. I recommend buying the 1-inch briquettes and using half a briquette at a time (you really don't need a whole briquette for a single spoonful of herbal incense). A briquette will burn for 45 minutes to 1 hour, and burning a spoonful of herbal incense doesn't take long at all. Simply snap the charcoal tablet in half, and save one half for another time.

A single spoonful of incense is usually all you'll need to release its energy into your space. A scant teaspoonful sprinkled on a glowing charcoal will release a cloud of smoke. Unlike stick incense, herbal incense burns all at once until it is gone, and thus releases more smoke and scent over a shorter period of time. The energy and scent linger in the space, however, so there's no need to keep piling on the incense blend to produce a steady supply of smoke. If you try to burn too much incense, the room will become too smoky and it's likely to set off your smoke detector.

*This is NOT barbecue charcoal.

With herbal incense, a little goes a long way. When you use herbal incense, you're actually smoldering it, not burning it—there's no flame involved. The bits of resin melt and the herbal matter turns black and crackles away. If you choose to use matches to light the charcoal, long-stemmed matches are preferable because short safety matches burn down too quickly. A long-handled barbecue lighter is ideal for lighting charcoal briquettes.

Here are the steps to burning your incense:

1. Hold the charcoal in one hand with a pair of tweezers or a small pair of tongs while you apply the flame to the charcoal with your other hand. (Remember that if your tweezers or tongs are metal they will conduct the heat of the charcoal briquette once it begins to ignite.)

2. Hold the flame to the edge of the briquette, and as it catches fire it will begin to sparkle. If your charcoal is particularly quick, those sparkles will begin to move across the surface of the briquette, firing the rest of the surface. If your charcoal is very densely made or slightly damp because of humidity in the environment, you may have to hold the flame to different areas to light as many as possible before they combine to ignite the rest of the briquette.

3. When the briquette has fully ignited, lay it down carefully on the layer of sand or earth in your censer. You can use almost any heatproof dish as a censer, as long as it has a layer of material to absorb the heat of the charcoal. To be on the safe side, you can put a trivet or heatproof coaster under your censer to protect your table or altar from heat damage.

continued

continued

4. Wait until the sparkles have finished coursing across the surface of the briquette and the surface has begun to glow faintly red.

5. At this point, your charcoal is ready to receive a teaspoonful of herbal incense or a pinch of resin. Some people prefer to wait until there is a thin layer of gray ash on top of the briquette before sprinkling incense on it.

6. Sprinkle the herbal incense gently on the charcoal briquette, visualizing the goal for which you've created the blend. Don't just pile a heaping spoonful of the incense on the charcoal briquette. A solid chunk of incense can smother the charcoal briquette.

7. When the incense has finished burning, you can wait 15 or 20 minutes for the smoke to dissipate a bit, then sprinkle another ½ teaspoon of incense on the charcoal.

8. When this has burned away, leave the charcoal to burn out on its own. It will turn to gray ash. Allow this ash to cool, then stir it gently into the sand or earth in your censer.

Keeping a small bottle of water or a second bowl of earth or sand nearby to smother the charcoal and incense should it somehow get out of control is always an intelligent precaution.

SPELL BAGS

Spell bags, small fabric bags into which you place a variety of objects and items chosen for their magical associations, are used in various magical applications. Spell bags can be made in any size and used anywhere. You can hang one above the door, tuck one into your car's glove compartment, tuck them in drawers, handbags, hang them on bedposts...the only limit is your imagination.

Following is a basic, small protection charm project. Use it as a basis for creating your own. Remember to use dried herbs in bags and pillows; fresh plant matter will rot.

Protection Charm

This spell bag is designed to be hung above your front or back door, whichever is used more frequently. By using a tie on the spell bag, you can open it and add other items as needed to supplement the magical energy. Spell bags can also be sewn shut, like small pillows, although if this is done they should not be opened.

If there comes a time when the spell bag is no longer required, or if the usefulness is past, then undo or unpick the spell bag and separate the items inside. Dispose of them separately, adding the herbs to your garden or compost.

YOU WILL NEED

2 (3 × 5-inch) pieces of red or black fabric

Iron (optional)

Thread to match

Needle

Pins

1 (12-inch) length of red yarn or narrow ribbon

1 snowflake obsidian

1 teaspoon caraway seeds

1 teaspoon mugwort

Pinch of salt

STEPS TO TAKE

1. Make a small hem along one of the short sides of the fabric rectangle as follows: Fold the edge of one of the 3-inch-long sides of one cloth rectangle down ¼ inch, wrong side to wrong side, and press into place with your fingers or the iron. Using a running stitch, sew the edge down. Repeat on the other piece of cloth.

2. Place the cloth rectangles face-to-face, right side to right side, matching edges. (The folded edge will be facing out on both.) Pin into place.

3. Using a running stitch, sew along the three raw edges of the rectangle. Leave the side with the hems open. Turn the pouch right side out.

4. Fold the yarn or ribbon in half. Secure the fold to the outside of one of the side seams of the pouch with a couple of small stitches.

5. Into this small pouch, place the snowflake obsidian and the herbs.

6. Tie the spell bag shut with the yarn or ribbon. Hang from a small nail above your door.

DREAM PILLOWS

Another form of spell bag, the dream pillow allows the gentle energies of the herbs to interact with your own energy while you sleep. Tuck the dream pillow under your bed pillow, hang it on your bedpost, or set it on your bedside table. An ideal way to reinforce the magical goal of the herbs in the dream pillow is to choose cloth of an appropriate color you associate with the magical goal. If you add a ribbon to the pillow for hanging, choose an appropriate length to slip over the bedpost. Here are some suggested blends for dream pillows:

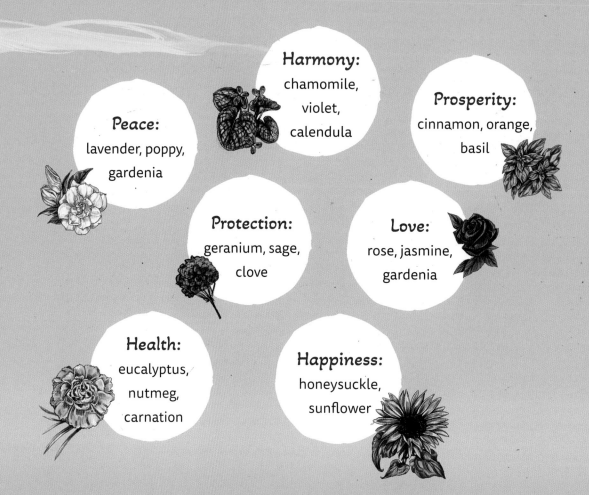

Harmony: chamomile, violet, calendula

Prosperity: cinnamon, orange, basil

Peace: lavender, poppy, gardenia

Protection: geranium, sage, clove

Love: rose, jasmine, gardenia

Health: eucalyptus, nutmeg, carnation

Happiness: honeysuckle, sunflower

Sweet Dreams Pillow

Another form of spell bag, the dream pillow allows the gentle energies of the herbs to interact with your own energy while you sleep. Tuck the dream pillow under your bed pillow, hang it on your bedpost, or set it on your bedside table.

YOU WILL NEED

1 tablespoon violets

1 tablespoon spearmint

2 tablespoons lavender

Small bowl

1 (8 × 4-inch) rectangle of cloth (your choice of color)

Thread to match

Pins

Needle

Iron (optional)

Cotton batting (about the size of your fist, or 2 [4 × 4-inch] squares)

Ribbon (optional; for length, see cotton batting)

continued

continued

STEPS TO TAKE

1. Blend the herbs in the bowl with your fingertips.
2. Fold the rectangle of cloth over onto itself so that you have a square of doubled material. If you are using a fabric with a design, make sure the design is on the inside. Pin the two halves together.
3. Using a running stitch, sew along two of the three open sides of the fabric square, leaving one side open.
4. Fold approximately ¼ inch of the raw edge of the open side down on what is currently the outside of the pouch. Finger-press the edge so that it stays creased, or use the iron. Turn the fabric pouch right side out, so that the seams are to the inside. (The raw edge of the pressed side should be inside the pouch.)
5. Tease out your cotton or cotton batting so it is fluffier and larger. Place the herbs in the center of the cotton and fold the edges inward so that the herbs are rolled inside the cotton. If the cotton batting is flat, lay one of the squares down, pour the herbs in the middle, lay the second square on top, and secure all four sides with a running stitch.
6. Tuck the herbs in the cotton batting inside the fabric pouch. Pin the open side closed. If you are adding a ribbon hanger, fold your piece of ribbon and insert the ends into the open side of the pouch and pin them into place. Sew the pillow closed with a running stitch, sewing the ribbon into place as you go.
7. Tuck your new dream pillow under your bed pillow or place it next to your pillow before you sleep.

You can increase the size of this pillow. The larger you make it, however, the more cotton batting you will need to protect the herbs inside. You may use as many or as few herbs as you like.

Ritual Brooms

In Chapter 2 you learned how to use a broom to purify an area.
Finding a natural-bristle broom can be a challenge. But making her
own tools is a time-honored practice for a witch of any kind, and
making a broom is particularly easy. Gather twigs and a longer stick
from below the trees where you live so your broom is a tool tied into
the energy of your particular geographic location. Mixed with your
own personal energy, this natural energy will create a broom vibrating
with green witch power! Try to identify the trees from which you
gather your twigs. The more you know about your supplies, the more
tuned into their energy you'll be.

If you have trees on your own land, save twigs and a long stick
during your annual pruning. Otherwise, you can usually walk
residential streets in the fall and gather twigs from the piles
of pruned material lying on the curbside for pickup. Ask the
resident's permission to take the branches and twigs. If the
wood you pick up is wet, allow it to dry in a protected,
ventilated space, such as a garage or your basement,
for a couple of weeks.

Your broom can be custom-made to reflect your personality.
Attach feathers or shells or stones, carve it, or tie charms
onto the broom with twine. Use symbols meaningful to
you that will enhance the broom's positive energy.

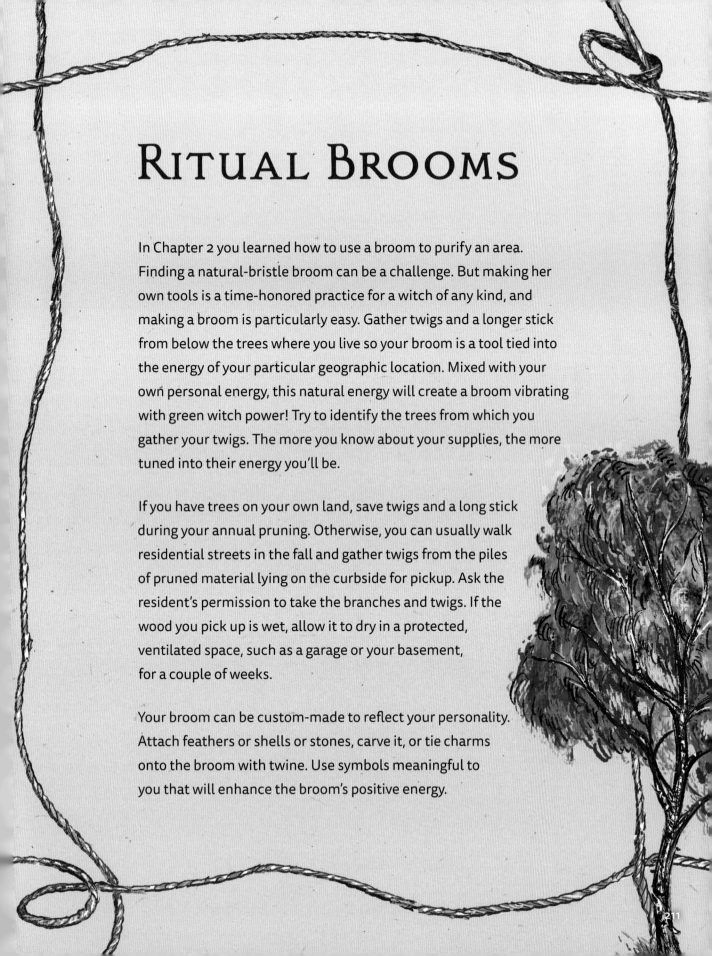

Create a Twig Broom

When making your broom, it is important to wind the leather tightly around the twigs. The tension is part of what keeps the twigs on the end of the broom.

YOU WILL NEED

Work gloves (optional)

Newspaper

1 stout stick, approximately 5 feet long, between ¾ and 1 inch in diameter

Saw (optional)

Sandpaper

Twigs approximately 18 inches long, no thicker than ¼ inch each*

Wood glue

Leather strip, 5 feet long, at least ¾ inch wide

4 finishing nails

Hammer

STEPS TO TAKE

1. Cover your work area with newspaper.
2. Take the 5-foot stick and decide which end will be the top of the handle and which end will be the sweeping end. If the stick has bark on it, decide whether you wish to strip it off or keep it on. If you're using a branch broken off a tree, you may wish to saw the top end flat. Sand the top end of the handle so that no sharp edges or splinters remain.

*Enough to make a 3-inch pile when you gather them together in your hands.

3. Sort through the pile of smaller sticks and cut or break off any that have other twigs sticking out at odd angles. Either by hand or with the saw, trim them all to roughly 18 inches long.

4. Take one of the thicker twigs and set it against the bottom end of the broom's handle. Overlap the ends of the twig and the broom handle so that approximately 5–6 inches of the twig is lying against the bottom 5 inches of the broom. (The twig will extend about a foot past the end of the broom.) Dot wood glue along those overlapping 5 inches and press the twig against the broom. Laying one end of the leather strip across the twig, add a drop of wood glue to secure it to the wood. Holding it together firmly, hammer one of the finishing nails through the leather strip and the twig into the broom.

5. Spread a thin layer of glue around the bottom 5 inches of the broom and begin to add additional 18-inch twigs, overlapping the top 5–6 inches of each twig against the bottom 5 inches of the broom. Place the second twig over the leather strip, then the next twig under it. Make sure you maintain a consistent tension on the leather strip.

6. When you reach the first twig again, dot some more glue along the top 5 inches of the first layer of twigs and continue adding more twigs, still alternating the leather strip above and below twigs. Remember to keep the twigs wrapped tight. Don't worry about making sure the ends of the twigs are perfectly even. This is a handmade broom and a tool of magic designed to sweep air and energy, not an even floor. It doesn't have to be perfect.

continued

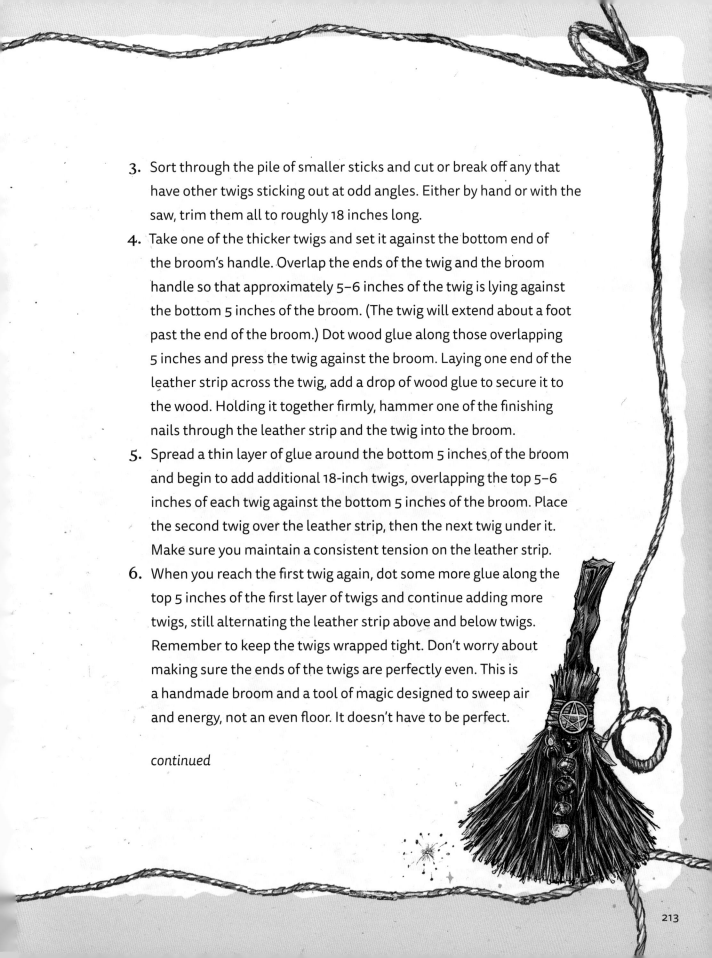

continued

7. When you have reached the halfway point of the second layer, opposite where you started, hold the leather taut and hammer a second finishing nail through it and the twig into the first layer of twigs and the handle below. Continue adding twigs.

8. Continue adding the twigs to the broom, dotting more wood glue along the tops of the twigs as you begin another layer. Keep winding the leather over and under the twigs.

9. When you are satisfied with the thickness of the twig end of the broom, or when you come to the end of your pile of twigs, hammer another nail into the leather and the twigs through to the broom handle. Dot more glue along the inside of the rest of the leather strip and wrap the leather around and around the twigs. Pull it tight. Secure the end of the leather with a final dot of glue and one final nail.

10. Allow the broom to rest flat (not dangling) on a table or floor for at least 36 hours, or until the glue has completely dried. If you wish to further decorate your broom by winding leather around the handle, adding feathers or shells or stones, or by carving it, do so when the glue is dry. You can also tie charms onto the broom with twine.

11. Before you use your new magical broom for the first time, empower it by holding it in your hands and visualizing a sparkling white light glowing around it. See the sparkling energy being absorbed into the broom.

PERFUMED BALMS

This magical craft takes an essential oil of your choice and makes it a solid balm, which can be used as a magical perfume. The term "balm" indicates comfort of some kind, as well as a solid substance that melts when applied to the warmth of the skin. A few things to remember about balms:

1.

Make sure the jar, tin, or container you choose to contain the balm has a wide enough mouth for you to reach inside with your fingers. Choose a container that isn't too deep and make sure that the lid closes tightly to preserve the contents as long as possible.

2.

Carefully research the oils you wish to use. You don't want to use too much of an oil, like cinnamon, that can irritate your skin. Always consider your skin's sensitivity.

3.

When applying the balm, use a small amount. Scoop up a bit on your fingertip and rub it gently with a circular motion where you wish to apply it. Do not allow the balm to come in contact with your eyes. Wash your hands after use or after the ritual activity you wish to be enhanced by the balm. In the summer, keep your balm in the fridge for a cooling sensation when you apply it.

4.

Balms should not be applied to the skin of children.

Magical Balm

Remember to label the tin or container clearly with the name of the balm. Write the recipe in your green witch journal.

YOU WILL NEED

1½ teaspoons beeswax beads

¼ cup sweet almond oil or jojoba oil

Small, clean, empty can

Saucepan and water

5–9 drops essential oil(s) of your choice

1 teaspoon vitamin E oil (optional)

Chopstick or Popsicle stick

Small jar or container with lid

STEPS TO TAKE

1. Place the beeswax beads and the almond or jojoba oil in the uncovered can. Place the can in a saucepan filled half-full with water to create a double boiler. This keeps the flammable oils from coming into direct contact with the heat source. Set the saucepan on the stove over medium heat.

2. Allow the heat of the water to melt the beeswax and almond or jojoba oil.

3. Remove the saucepan from the stove. Wearing oven mitts to protect your hands, remove the can from the water bath.

4. Swirl in the drops of essential oil and the vitamin E oil. As you do this, empower the mixture with your magical intent.

5. Allow the mixture to cool slightly. As it cools, the surface will solidify. Using a chopstick or a Popsicle stick, stir it gently to recombine the solid with the liquid. As you stir, reinforce your magical intent.

6. When the mixture has cooled but before it is completely solid, pour it into the clean jar or container and seal it. Label it with the contents and the date. To use the balm, scoop a small amount onto a fingertip and smooth onto your skin.

Here are suggestions for balms:

Meditation Balm

3 drops of lavender

3 drops of sandalwood

2 drops of violet

Rub a small amount into your temples and the inside of your wrists. This is also an excellent blend to use for relaxation and to aid sleep.

Purification Balm

2 drops of lavender

3 drops of frankincense

3 drops of jasmine

Dot a small amount on your third eye (in the center of your forehead), on your chest, and on the solar plexus. Use whenever you wish to clear negative emotion or energy from your emotional or physical body.

Love Balm

3 drops of rose

3 drops of jasmine

2 drops of lavender

1 drop of vanilla

Dot on the inside of your wrists, over your heart, at the nape of your neck, and behind your knees.

Abundance Balm

1 drop of cinnamon

2 drops of orange

3 drops of mint

2 drops of pine

Rub a small amount in the palms of your hands and on the soles of your feet.

Healing Balm

2 drops of rosemary

2 drops of eucalyptus

2 drops of myrrh

2 drops of sandalwood

This balm can be used for spiritual, emotional, and physical healing. This is particularly good used on the chest or back. Avoid using this balm near eyes or sensitive skin, because rosemary and eucalyptus can be irritating.

CHAPTER 8

BECOME
a Natural
HEALER

There are deep spiritual benefits to walking the path of the green witch. By immersing yourself in the energy of the planet and its flora, you can achieve higher levels of consciousness, which will benefit all those you interact with and the environment in which you live. One of the green witch's goals is to heal others, but remember that it is never wise to just give out teas or other preparations unless you are trained as a qualified herbalist. This is especially true if the preparation is intended for major or chronic problems. If someone comes to you complaining of an upset stomach or a headache, however, you can use your judgment and the folk knowledge you possess and have noted in your journal to suggest a treatment.

The Steps of Healing

Green witches are natural healers who seek to soothe the world around them. Healing is the rebalancing of energies that have become disturbed. Each step must be experienced in fullness and in time. This goes for healing the earth as well as yourself, other individuals, and the community. You have to learn from the process so that each step is thoroughly felt, understood, and completed. There are two steps to healing:

1.

Cleansing and/or purifying of the negative presence

2.

Replacing the negative presence with something positive

Many people focus on the first step and forget about the second. Nature abhors a vacuum, and what results from the first step is an empty space where the negative energy was and which new energy will rush to fill. We do not always control what kind of energy fills that space. To gain control and finish the healing process properly, perform a blessing (which asks another entity or spirit to bestow positive energy) or channel positive energy yourself to strengthen the object or person being healed. Be wary, however, of channeling energy that has already been programmed until you know exactly what your subject needs. You may assume your subject needs strength, but the actual need may be different. Filling the empty space with plain, unprogrammed, positive energy is safer. It allows the body to use it for whatever it requires.

Healing Teas

A tea is a potion that can be consumed. Usually made with water, the basic technique for preparing a tea is by infusion if you're using leaves or flowers, or decoction if you're using denser herbal material, such as roots, stems, twigs, or bark.

There are many teas available on the market today designed for certain therapeutic benefits such as stress relief, better sleep, headache relief, and so forth. While you can certainly use these commercial teas, when you create your own you know exactly what is going into them. You can also avoid herbs to which you are sensitive and use herbs you prefer. The following recipes may be made with fresh or dry herbs. If using fresh herbs, increase the amount of plant matter to 1 tablespoon per cup of boiling water for a single serving and make only enough for as many servings as you intend to prepare right away. Fresh blends cannot be stored.

Remember that taking anything internally without researching it can be dangerous. These recipes are not intended to be used as authoritative medical advice; they are offered here as folk wisdom.

Herbal Teas

Marshmallow Tea

This tea soothes a sore throat or digestive problems. Its magical associations are protection and healing. Makes 1 cup.

  1 tablespoon (⅔ ounce) dried chopped marshmallow root

  1 cup water

1. Place marshmallow root in water.
2. Bring to a simmer, and simmer for 10 minutes.
3. Remove from heat and allow to steep for another 10 minutes.
4. Strain and drink.
5. Take as necessary throughout the day.

Digestive Tea

This tea treats an upset stomach. Its magical association is prosperity. 1 teaspoon of the tea blend makes 1 cup of tea.

  1 part peppermint

  1 part basil

  1 part dill seed

  1 cup boiling water

1. Mix dry herbs in a small jar.
2. To brew, pour 1 cup of boiling water over 1 teaspoon of the herbal blend.
3. Steep 7–10 minutes. Strain and drink.

Cold Tea

This tea is for the treatment of colds. Its magical associations are energy and healing. 1 teaspoon of the tea blend makes 1 cup of tea.

> 1 part ginger
>
> 1 part elderflowers
>
> 1 part yarrow
>
> 1 cup boiling water

1. Mix dry herbs in a small jar.
2. To brew, pour 1 cup of boiling water over 1 teaspoon of the herbal blend.
3. Steep 5–7 minutes. Strain and drink.

Bedtime Tea

This tea is good for aiding sleep. Its magical associations are peace, harmony, healing, love, and happiness. 1 teaspoon of the tea blend makes 1 cup of tea.

> 1 part lavender
>
> 1 part catnip
>
> 1 part verbena
>
> 1 part chamomile
>
> 1 cup boiling water

1. Mix dry herbs in a small jar.
2. To brew, pour 1 cup of boiling water over 1 teaspoon of the herbal blend.
3. Steep 5–7 minutes. Strain and drink.

Love Tea

This tea is for relaxation and celebrating love. Its magical associations are love, happiness, peace, and harmony. 1 teaspoon of the tea blend makes 1 cup of tea.

> 1 part rose petals
>
> 1 part lavender
>
> 1 part jasmine
>
> Pinch of cinnamon (optional)
>
> 1 cup boiling water

1. Mix dry herbs in a small jar.
2. To brew, pour 1 cup of boiling water over 1 teaspoon of the herbal blend.
3. Steep 5–7 minutes. Strain and drink.

Steeped Healing Honey

This lemon- and ginger-steeped honey is good for helping to soothe sore throats and other cold and flu symptoms as well as supporting the immune system in general. Try to find local raw honey to use. This honey will keep for around a month in the refrigerator. To extend its shelf life, you can stir in 3 tablespoons of brandy.

Honey is acidic, so to avoid this project corroding metal canning lids, look for plastic lids, usually found in the same section of the store as other canning goods. Alternatively, you can place a square of waxed paper over the mouth of the jar, and then screw the lid into place.

You can also experiment with steeping other ingredients in this basic blend. Add turmeric and/or cinnamon for their anti-inflammatory properties. You can also replace some of the lemon and ginger with crushed garlic and/or some diced onion, if you want more power and don't mind the taste.

Adults and children over the age of five can take this steeped honey by the spoonful as needed for sore throats, coughs, and cold and flu symptoms. It's also delicious stirred into tea or plain hot water for a soothing drink.

Honey
Mason jar (8-ounce or 1-cup size)
1 medium lemon, seeded and thinly sliced
Fresh ginger root (approximately a 1-inch piece), roughly chopped

1. Spoon or pour a thin layer of honey in the bottom of the Mason jar.
2. Lay a lemon slice in the honey, then one or two chunks of ginger. Cover with a layer of honey.
3. Repeat honey-lemon and ginger-honey layers until about 1 inch from the top of the jar. Fill up the remaining space with honey.
4. Cap with a plastic top (or layer of waxed paper between metal lid and jar) to prevent corrosion. Store in the refrigerator for approximately one month.

Energy-Empowering Essential Oils

An oil is a handy way to carry the essence of an herb or other natural object. The basic ways to prepare an oil are by enfleurage or by maceration. If you prepare your own oils, they will carry the added benefit of already being attuned to you and your personal energy, although you should still empower them before use as you do with any supplies. Not everyone can prepare a full stock of as many oils as they would like to have. Two kinds of oils are generally available for purchase from shops:

1.

Essential oils, which carry the pure essence of the plant in a carrier oil.

2.

Perfume oils, which are artificially scented.

Most green witches like to use as pure a product as possible
in their work and will therefore choose an essential oil over a
perfume oil. An essential oil is prepared directly from the original
plant, which means that when you use it in magical or medicinal
work it is guaranteed to carry the original energy of the plant
along with its chemical benefits.

An essential oil is more expensive than perfume oil, but it will also
be stronger; only a drop or two is necessary to involve the energy
of the plant. The scent of a perfume oil is less accurate than in
an essential oil and does not carry the plant's energy signature.
Although irresponsible merchants sometimes attempt to sell
artificial perfume oils as essential oils, the comparative prices are
a good guide to identifying what is essential and what is perfume.

Whether you create your own personal oil blend or use a blend
made from the following recipes, you can add a drop or two
to any project you undertake for that magical
purpose to add extra energy and power.

Reminder: Remember to dilute pure essential
oils with a light carrier oil if you plan to use
them on your skin. If adding them to a recipe like
those in this chapter, such as bath salts or salves,
you don't need to dilute them first, as the other
ingredients serve that purpose.

Personal Oil Blend

Creating an oil specifically to represent yourself and your energy gives you a bottled essence that can be used for a multitude of purposes.

Oils (your choice)

Small dishes, bowls, or empty vials

Container with tight-fitting lid for the final oil blend

1. The recipe for this blend is really up to you. Think about your favorite herbs, flowers, and trees. Think about the elements you resonate with. Think about the color of the plants the oils are derived from and the scent.

2. In your green witch notebook, make up a list of these elements. You don't have to limit them to oils you already have on hand. Also think about the emotions or goals you wish to include in your blend. Are you creative? Are you an excellent communicator? Are you a nurturer?

3. Next, look up correspondences for the plants on your list, then look up plants that correspond to the traits and goals on your list. Write this information in your journal.

4. Now start to narrow the list down. Use your intuition and consider the importance of what corresponds to what.

5. When you have a manageable list of between three and thirteen items, work out your proportions. How much of each oil? To begin, you may wish to blend everything in a proportion of one part each. You can also use one oil as a base and add only trace amounts of others. However you mix your personal oil, the way you put it together is up to you.

6. When you've worked out your proportions, take a look at your stock of oils. If you're missing oils, decide whether you will make them yourself (which will require time) or buy them. You will also need to decide whether you will use essential oils or perfume oils. Remember, you can mix these oils together.

7. To blend your personal oil, measure out the appropriate proportions of your chosen oils and place each in an individual small dish or clean, empty vial.

8. One by one, pour the oils into your chosen container. Swirl them together.

9. Empower the final oil blend by holding it in your hands and visualizing your personal energy flowing from your hands into the oil. Continue until you feel the oil has been fully empowered with your energy.

10. Cover and label your personal oil blend. Write down the date, the final ingredients, and the proportions in your green witch journal.

Oil Recipes

Following are oil recipes that you can use. They may also inspire you to create new recipes. Do not take these oils internally! Blend the oils by following steps 7 through 10 in the previous Personal Oil Blend recipe. If the recipe calls for an addition of herbal matter, add it last.

Awake and Alive Oil

The magical associations of this oil are happiness, health, protection, and energy.

1 part rosemary	½ part lemon
1 part mint	½ part thyme
1 part orange	

Patience

The magical associations of this oil are peace, harmony, and love.

1 part rose	1 part pine
1 part lavender	

Prosperity

The magical associations of this oil are movement and energy.

1 part mint	1 part cinnamon
1 part basil	1 part pine

Health

This oil's magical associations are health, communication, and strength.

1 part thyme

1 part eucalyptus

1 part pine

1 part ginger

Peace

The magical associations of this oil are meditation, spirituality, and harmony.

1 part violet

1 part lavender

1 part jasmine

1 part sandalwood

Protection

This oil's magical associations are protection, wisdom, and purification.

1 part sage

1 part sandalwood

1 part angelica

1 clove

Pinch of salt

Love

The magical associations of this oil are love and harmony.

1 part rose

1 part jasmine

½ part geranium

¼ part vanilla

Infused Oils

The four basic methods of extracting benefits from plant matter—infusion, decoction, enfleurage, and maceration—were introduced in the previous chapter. Here's how to prepare infused oils via enfleurage, to be used in things like balms and salves, recipes for which will follow. Remember, infused oils aren't essential oils; they won't have as strong a scent or as concentrated an effect, but they're still fine for magical work. Good oils to use include sweet almond, jojoba, and grapeseed. Olive oil is good for infusing cooking oils.

Enfleurage can be done either hot or cold. Cold infusion is as easy as pouring room-temperature oil over a jar half-filled with dry plant matter and leaving it in a cool, dry place to steep for four to six weeks, shaking it every week or so, then straining it. In general, I need infused oils more quickly than that, so I use one of the following two warm infusion methods. I also prefer warm enfleurage because heat does a better job extracting the important parts of the plant matter, especially if it's thick or has firm cell walls. A key thing to remember is to keep the temperature of your oil under 120°F. Ideally, your target temperature is around 100°F. You're warming the oil, not cooking the plant matter.

Oven Enfleurage

This warm infusion method is created in your oven and takes a bit of time to make—approximately 4–6 hours, depending on the plant matter you are using.

Plant matter	Spoon
Oil	Cheesecloth
Ovenproof dish	Two jars or bottles with lids

1. Preheat the oven to 100°F.
2. Place the plant matter and the oil into the ovenproof dish. Stir with the spoon to ensure that all the plant matter is coated with oil. Make sure there are no bubbles.
3. Set the dish with the oil and herbs into the oven. Cook for 4–6 hours, uncovered (less time for delicate flowers or plant matter; more time for woody or thicker plant matter).
4. When you're ready to remove the oil, turn off the heat and remove the dish from the oven.
5. Allow it to cool. Strain the cooled oil through cheesecloth into a clean, dry jar, and compost the plant matter. Cover the container and allow it to sit until the oil is clear. This resting period allows any sediment that made it through the filtering process to settle to the bottom of the container.
6. Decant the clean oil into the final container, discarding the sediment. Screw on the lid and label.

Stovetop Enfleurage

This warm infusion method is created on your stovetop and takes less than an hour to make.

> Double boiler (a bain-marie, or a saucepan and a metal bowl
> that can rest atop it)
> Water
> Plant matter
> Oil
> Spoon
> Thermometer
> Cheesecloth
> Two jars or bottles with lids

1. Fill the saucepan halfway with water and set it on the stove.
2. In the top part of the double boiler or the bowl, place the plant matter and the oil. Stir with the spoon to coat all the herbs and remove any air bubbles.
3. Set the top of the double boiler or the metal bowl on the pot with water. Set the heat at medium-low, or whatever level your stove requires to keep water at a simmer.

4. Simmer for approximately 45 minutes (less time for delicate herbs, more for woody or thicker plant matter). Check the level of the water in the lower pot to make sure it doesn't go dry; be careful not to get any steam or water drops in the oil when you do. Use the thermometer to check the temperature of the oil in the upper pot or bowl to make sure it stays around 100°F, and doesn't pass 120°F.

5. When you're ready to remove the oil, turn off the heat and remove the top of the double boiler or the bowl. Allow it to cool. Strain the cooled oil through cheesecloth into a clean, dry jar, and compost the plant matter. Cover the container and allow it to sit. This resting period allows any sediment that made it through the filtering process to settle to the bottom of the container.

6. Decant the clean oil into the final container, discarding the sediment. Screw on the lid and label.

REGENERATING BATHS

A bath is a magical thing. Water itself is a healing and soothing element, and when you add herbs to it you can create a wide range of effects.

To avoid having leaves and stems and other little bits of green matter floating around in your tub and clogging the drain, you can make an infusion or a decoction and pour it into your bathwater. You can also put a couple of spoonfuls of an herbal blend inside a cotton sock, put a knot in it, and toss it in under the running water as you fill the tub. The result is an infusion brewed directly in your bath. Remove the sock before you get in, or leave it to further strengthen the infusion while you bathe. When you remove it, hang it up and allow it to dry, then undo the tie and turn it inside out to brush away the dried herbal matter so you can reuse it whenever you need to.

Alternatively, you can make a reusable bath sachet by sewing two washcloths together on three sides, leaving the top open. Sew 12 inches of ribbon or string to one side seam about one third of the way down. Place your spoonfuls of dried or fresh herbs inside (no more than ½ cup), then gather the open end and tie the pouch closed by wrapping the ribbon or string around it firmly and tying a bow. You can hang this bath sachet under the faucet as the water runs or toss it in and allow it to soak.

You can also use oils in your bath. If you are using essential oils, make sure you use only three drops total. Any more can irritate your skin or overwhelm your system. Remember, essential oils are concentrated extracts that carry chemicals. It's easy to overdose on them. If you prefer to bathe with lots of oil, blend those three drops into a ¼ cup of a carrier oil, such as jojoba or sweet almond oil, then pour all the oil into your bath. I recommend that you do this with both essential and perfume oils because your skin may be sensitive to both. Adding a few drops to a carrier oil makes for a safer bathing experience.

For a different sort of bath, blend the drops of oil into 1 cup of milk and pour that into the running water.

BATH SALTS

Bath salts are a lovely way to relax and absorb magical energy at the same time. Salt is a naturally purifying substance that also helps relax tense muscles. When a bath salt recipe calls for salt, however, it doesn't mean table salt. Epsom salts, sea salt, kosher salt, or a combination should be used.

You can blend and store your bath salts in Mason jars, but the salt can corrode the metal lids. So, look for jars with glass lids fitted with plastic seals, jars with snap-down lids, or jars with cork tops. Never store bath salts in a metal tin or it will rust, and be aware that a plastic container will tend to absorb the scent of the salts, which makes it difficult to reuse.

In general, use 1 tablespoon to ¼ cup of these salts in your bath. If you prefer a lot of salt in your bath, increase the amount slowly to make sure you don't irritate your skin or system.

Basic Bath Salt Recipe

Use this recipe as a basis for your own magical bath salts. You can use any combination of sea salt, Epsom salts, and kosher salt. Makes 4 cups (32 ounces).

> 2 cups sea salt or other salts
>
> 2 cups baking soda
>
> Glass jar with tight-fitting lid, large enough to hold 32 ounces

1. Combine ingredients in blender or food processor. Blend until combined and reduced to a fine powder.
2. Store in a tightly lidded jar.
3. To use, pour ½ cup of the salts into the bath under running water.
4. To this basic recipe you can add any or all of the following:

   > 3–5 drops essential oil(s)
   >
   > 2 teaspoons finely ground dried herbs
   >
   > 1–3 drops food coloring
   >
   > 1 part finely ground oatmeal
   >
   > ½ part finely ground almonds

5. If your skin tends to be dry, add 1 teaspoon liquid glycerin (available in drugstores) to the bath to moisturize your skin.

Prosperity Bath Salts

Use this recipe when you feel you need to boost your personal prosperity energy. Makes 2½ cups (20 ounces).

  1 cup sea salt

  1 cup Epsom salts

  Glass jar with tight-fitting lid, large enough to hold 20 ounces

  3 drops orange oil

  2 drops cinnamon oil or 1 teaspoon ground cinnamon

  ¼ cup ground mint leaves

  3 drops green vegetable food coloring (optional)

1. Place the salts in a blender or food processor and blend until combined and reduced to a fine powder. Pour the salts into the jar and cap it. Shake to combine the salts.

2. Open the jar again. Add the drops of oil and the ground herbs. Cap the jar and shake well to blend.

3. If using food coloring, open the jar and add 3 drops. Cap and shake well to blend. Be aware that a little food coloring goes a long way; don't add much. If you want the color darker, add 1–2 more drops and blend again. The color is added simply to enhance the prosperity energy of the other ingredients. If you associate another color with prosperity, then by all means substitute it.

4. To use, pour ½ cup of the salts into your bath under running water.

MILK BATHS

There's something remarkably luxurious about adding milk to your bathwater. Milk has a wonderfully softening action on the skin. Do not, however, use milk baths if you are sensitive to dairy products.

This is the simplest recipe for a milk bath:

1. Take 1 cup of whole milk (don't use skim or even partially skim milk) and pour it into your bathwater.
2. For extra softening action, add 1 tablespoon of honey to the cup of milk and swirl it about to disperse it before pouring it into the water. If you like, you can warm the milk up first to help blend in the honey: heat the honey-milk mixture in the microwave for 1 minute.
3. You can also add a few drops of oil to the warm milk before pouring it into your bath. Swirling to combine the oil with the milk helps disperse the oil throughout the bathwater, instead of just letting it float on the surface of the water.

Oatmeal Milk Bath

The combination of oatmeal, a known skin softener, and milk in this bath blend makes for a deliciously soothing soak. Try it if you're sunburned or to soften rough skin. You can also add herbs or a couple of drops of oil to the following recipe. Makes 4 cups (32 ounces).

1 cup cornstarch

2 cups milk powder

1 cup dry oatmeal

Glass jar with tight-fitting lid, large enough to hold 32 ounces

1. Place all the ingredients in a blender or food processor. Blend to combine until reduced to a fine powder. Pour into jar.
2. To use, sprinkle ½ cup of the dry bath blend under the tap while running your bath.

Herbal Milk Bath

This basic and simple milk bath is an excellent base for any herbal addition, making it adaptable to any magical need. For extra softening, you can use the Oatmeal Milk Bath as a base. Makes 3 cups (24 ounces).

> 1 cup cornstarch
>
> 2 cups milk powder
>
> 2 tablespoons dry herbs
>
> Glass jar with tight-fitting lid, large enough to hold 24 ounces

1. Place all ingredients in a blender or food processor. Blend until combined and reduced to a fine powder. Pour into jar.
2. To use, add ½ cup of powder to bath under running water.
3. Here are suggested herbal blends to add to milk baths:

Winter Energy Bath: nutmeg, cinnamon, pinch of ginger

Spring Dawn Bath: lavender, jasmine, apple blossom

Summer Garden Bath: lavender, roses, verbena, pinch of orange zest

Autumn Bronze Bath: poppy, nutmeg, sandalwood

HEALING BALMS and SALVES

In Chapter 7 you learned about magical balms and salves made in small batches that were suitable for magical purposes. But what if you want to make a larger batch for physical therapeutic or healing purposes? The following recipes will help you.

Safety Note: Balms and ointments are good for about three months. Don't make too much at once, unless you plan to share it with others. If you notice odd smells or discoloration, dispose of it to be safe.

Healing Balm

This balm features calendula, which is a wonderful healer. It also has chamomile to soothe the skin and St. John's Wort for antiviral and antibacterial properties. Even the lavender essential oil has antifungal properties. You can use this conditioning balm as a lip or cuticle balm, or to soothe dry and itchy skin. After your first batch, you may want to adjust the amounts of beeswax, cocoa butter, or infused oil to create a texture or consistency you prefer. The recipe makes approximately ⅓ cup.

Double boiler (a bain-marie, or a saucepan and a metal bowl that can rest atop it)

¼ cup olive oil infused with equal parts calendula, chamomile, and St. John's Wort
   (see previous pages for how to infuse oils)

2 teaspoons cocoa butter

3 teaspoons grated beeswax or beeswax pastilles

Rubber spatula

6 drops lavender essential oil (or other healing-supportive essential oil; optional)

Wide-mouth Mason jar and lid, or tin (4-ounce or ½-cup size)

1. In the top part of the double boiler over simmering water, slowly heat the infused olive oil, cocoa butter, and beeswax until just melted, stirring slowly.
2. Remove from the heat and allow to cool for a few minutes. If you are using any essential oil, add the drops at this stage.
3. Pour the mixture into the canning jar or tin and allow to cool completely before screwing on the lid.
4. Label and date the jar. Keep in a cool, dry place. Use within three months.

Herbal Healing Salve

A salve is a softer kind of balm. This balm uses the healing properties of calendula, plantain, and comfrey for a powerhouse of recovery support. You can gently rub into bruises or (cleaned) scrapes, or light cuts that don't need to be covered. This recipe makes about 3 ounces.

Double boiler (a bain-marie, or a saucepan and a metal bowl that can rest atop it)

Rubber spatula

3 ounces sweet almond oil infused with plantain, calendula, and comfrey (84 ml)

1 tablespoon beeswax

3 drops lavender essential oil (optional)

Wide-mouth Mason jar and lid, or tin (4-ounce or ½-cup size)

1. In the top part of the double boiler over simmering water, slowly heat the infused oil and beeswax until just melted, stirring slowly.
2. Remove from the heat and allow to cool for a few minutes. If you are using any essential oil, add the drops at this stage.
3. Pour the mixture into the canning jar or tin and allow to cool completely before screwing on the lid.
4. Label and date the jar. Keep in a cool, dry place. Use within three months.

Warming Muscle Rub

This recipe calls for essential oils, not infused oils, and creates a stronger balm. It works well with massage for tired or strained muscles, or chronic muscle and joint pain. Peppermint has menthol, which provides a cooling sensation, and the eucalyptus is an anti-inflammatory and analgesic. The ginger, clove, and black pepper are all warming, and rosemary helps improve circulation.

Double boiler (a bain-marie, or a saucepan and a metal bowl that can rest atop it)

¼ cup olive oil or sweet almond oil

⅛ cup shea butter or cocoa butter

2 tablespoons grated beeswax or beeswax pastilles

Rubber spatula

30 drops peppermint essential oil

15 drops eucalyptus essential oil

25 drops ginger essential oil

10 drops rosemary essential oil

10 drops cardamom essential oil

10 drops black pepper essential oil

5 drops clove essential oil

Wide-mouth Mason jar and lid, or tin (4-ounce or ½-cup size)

1. In the top part of the double boiler over simmering water, slowly heat the oil, butter, and beeswax until just melted, stirring slowly.
2. Remove from the heat and allow to cool for a few minutes. Add the drops of essential oils and stir gently.
3. Pour the mixture into the canning jar or tin and allow to cool completely before screwing on the lid.
4. Label and date the jar. Keep in a cool, dry place. Use within three months.

RESTORATIVE ELIXIRS

Elixirs can be used to anoint objects, and also people, as long as they have not been made with toxic components. Herbal elixirs are a way of steeping plant matter in a sweet alcoholic base to extract and preserve the medicinal qualities. You can take them by the spoonful or mix them with tea or hot water. Not only do the honey and alcohol help extract, but the alcohol also stabilizes the elixir and the honey makes the elixir sweeter and easier to consume. Elixirs are shelf stable for at least a year. Remember to label and date your containers.

Here are the basic directions for making an herbal elixir. The proportions may seem vague, but it all depends on the size of jar you're using. The rough proportions* are:

- ½ jar fresh plant matter (⅓ jar if using dried)
- ⅓ jar of honey
- ⅓ jar of alcohol

*If it looks like those don't add up, it's because the liquid fills in the spaces between the fresh herbs better than it does the dried.

Basic Elixir

It's worth buying a good-quality alcohol to use when making elixirs. (I prefer brandy for these, but use what you like.) The adult dose for this elixir is 1 teaspoon daily.

> Mason jar and lid (8-ounce or 1-cup size)
> ½ cup chopped fresh herbs
> ⅓ cup local raw honey
> Spoon for mixing
> ⅓ cup brandy or vodka
> Cheesecloth
> Sieve
> Fresh bottle(s) for storing, preferably amber or opaque

1. Place ½ cup of freshly chopped plant matter in the jar.
2. Spoon or pour the honey into the jar. Stir well.
3. Pour in the alcohol and stir well again. You can taste the mixture at this point, but the taste will mellow and sweeten during its resting period while the mixture macerates.
4. Put on the lid and label the jar. Place the jar in a cool, dark place for three to four weeks.
5. When the time is up, open the jar. Strain the mixture through cheesecloth. Press on the plant matter to release as much extracted goodness as possible.
6. Transfer the elixir into a fresh bottle (or smaller bottles). Label them. Close tightly and keep in a cool, dark place.

Spring Elixir

This spring elixir is like a tonic. Traditional tonics were used after winter to help wake up a sluggish system after months of cold and reduced activity. They usually had high amounts of vitamin C, vitamin A, and mineral content. Spring tonics help circulation, stimulate the appetite, and get the body ready for a physically demanding season of prepping fields and sowing.

Spring greens tend to be bitter; the honey and brandy help make the bitterness of the plant matter palatable.

Prepare roughly chopped equal amounts of:

- Dandelion greens (harvested early, before flowering)
- Rhubarb stalks
- Wild onion (ramps, *Allium tricoccum*)
- Nettles
- Burdock root

Proceed as in the previous Basic Elixir directions. Transfer the elixir into a fresh bottle (or smaller bottles). Label it. Close tightly and keep in a cool, dark place.

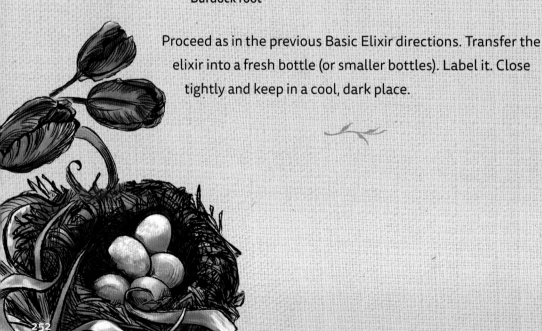

STONE ELIXIRS

Remember, many elixirs made with stones cannot be consumed internally. Stones and crystals are minerals, and while we usually think of them as inert, some stones have chemical compositions that are porous enough to physically leech into the water. Magical energies aren't the only things that can transfer to the liquid you're using to make an elixir! As a rule, any stone that has metal in its composition (such as copper, aluminum, iron, lead, and so forth) or has a soft composition (between 0 and 4 on the Mohs' scale of hardness) shouldn't be soaked in a liquid. Get a good crystal and gem reference book and look up the composition of the stones you want to use to select the best method.

Stones affect what they are near, and this effect is intensified when it is set up with intention. For these stones, here are alternate methods:

1.

Surround a glass container of the liquid to be charged with the stones.

2.

Set an empty glass in a bowl. Place the stone(s) in the glass. Pour the liquid to be charged into the bowl, around the base of the glass.

Use one of these methods to create stone elixirs such as the two that follow.

Stone Elixirs

Stone Elixir for Success

Aventurine

Amazonite

Carnelian

Citrine

Fluorite

Tiger's Eye

Stone Elixir to Enhance Intuition

Azurite

Apatite

Labradorite

Moonstone

Rutilated Quartz

Selenite

Magical Associations of NATURAL ITEMS

These lists of magical associations, like the other lists in this book, have been assembled over my years of practice and include both my own associations as well as traditional correspondences. Apart from personal experimentation and work, my sources over the years have included such books as Mrs. M. Grieve's *A Modern Herbal*, Scott Cunningham's *Encyclopedia of Magical Herbs*, Paul Beyerl's *The Master Book of Herbalism* and *A Compendium of Herbal Magick*, Jamie Wood's *The Wicca Herbal*, and the works of Amy Blackthorn and Juliet Diaz.

Allspice: prosperity, luck, healing, purification, protection, money

Almond: love, money, healing, wisdom

Angelica: protection, hex breaker, healing, psychic abilities, house blessing, purification

Anise: psychic abilities, lust, luck, purification, love

Apple: love, healing, peace

Ash: protection, strength, healing, prosperity

Basil: love, trust, abundance, prosperity, courage, discipline, protection, marriage, purification, luck, mental abilities

Bay: protection, purification, endurance, fidelity, psychic powers, divination, wisdom, strength

Bayberry: abundance, prosperity

Benzoin: purification, healing, prosperity

Birch: protection, purification, new beginnings, children

Catnip: cats, love, beauty, happiness, tranquility, luck

Cedar: healing, purification, protection, prosperity

Chamomile: purification, healing, soothes anxiety, gently heals bad luck, soothes children

Chickweed: animals, love, fidelity, healing, weight loss

Cinnamon: healing, love, lust, success, purification, protection, money, psychic awareness

Cinquefoil (five-finger grass): eloquence, cunning, money, protection, sleep, prophetic dreams, purification, love

Clove: protection, mental abilities, attraction, purification, comfort

Clover: lust, hex breaking, prosperity, purification, love, luck, protection, success, fidelity, comfort

Comfrey (boneset): healing, prosperity, protection, travel

Coriander: healing, love, lust

Cumin: protection, antitheft, love, fidelity

Cypress: protection, comfort, healing

Daisy: nature spirits, love, children

Dandelion: longevity, enhances psychic abilities, intuition, spiritual and emotional cleanser

Dill: protection, love, attraction, money, strength, luck, eases sleep, mental abilities, weight loss

Echinacea: healing

Elder, elderflower: protection from lightning, beauty, divination, prosperity, purification, house blessing, healing, sleep

Elm: love, protection

Eucalyptus: protection, healing

Eyebright: truth, pierces through illusion, certainty, psychic abilities

Fennel: courage, strength, cleansing

Feverfew: love, fidelity, protection, healing

Flax: money, protection, beauty, healing

Gardenia: love, attraction, peace, meditation

Garlic: healing, house blessing, protection, lust, antitheft

Geranium: love, healing, protection, fertility

Ginger: healing, love, money, energy

Hawthorn: protection, fertility, happiness

Hazel: mental abilities, fertility, protection, wisdom, luck

Heather: protection, rain, luck

Heliotrope: clairvoyance, psychic abilities, health, money

Hibiscus: love, lust, divination, harmony, peace

Honeysuckle: abundance, luck, prosperity, eases sorrow, enhances psychic abilities (do not use the berries; they are poisonous)

Hops: healing, sleep

Hyacinth: love, comfort, protection

Hyssop: purification, protection

Jasmine: love, attraction, prosperity, tranquility

Juniper: cleansing, purification, protection against accidents, protection against illness, love, antitheft, fertility, psychic abilities

Lavender: healing, love, happiness, heals grief and guilt, sleep, tranquility, protection, purification, peace, house blessing, wisdom, children, marriage

Lemon: purification, love, protection, happiness

Licorice: love, lust, protection, fidelity

Lilac: protection, beauty, love, psychic abilities, purification, prosperity

Lily: protection, love antidote, truth

Lime: love, purification, luck, sleep

Lotus: blessing, meditation, protection

Maple: sweetness, prosperity, marriage, love, money

Marigold: positive energy, protection, eases legal stress, increases psychic awareness, peace

Marjoram: protection, love, happiness, health, money, marriage, comfort

Meadowsweet: peace, love, happiness, psychic awareness

Mint: purification, preserves health, clarity of mind, protects travelers, attracts money, health, love, success

Mistletoe: healing, protection, love, fertility, sleep, luck

Mugwort: divination, protection, healing, strength, lust, psychic power, fertility, protects travelers

Nettle: cleansing, protects from danger, protects health

Nutmeg: clairvoyance, health, luck, fidelity

Oak: purification, protection, prosperity, health and healing, money, fertility, luck, strength

Onion: healing, protection, purification

Orange: love, joy, purification, prosperity

Oregano: peace

Parsley: healing, lust, fertility, love, passion, protection, hex breaker, prosperity, purification, protection, eases grief

Patchouli: money, fertility, lust, clairvoyance, divination, love, attraction

Pepper: protection, purification

Pine: prosperity, healing, purification, fertility

Poppy: fertility, abundance, sleep, love

Rose: healing, love, conciliation, restoration, self-love, attracts love and good fortune, heals trouble, enhances psychic abilities

Rosemary: cleansing, protection, healing, longevity, improves memory and concentration

Rowan (mountain ash): purification, house blessing, protection, healing, psychic abilities, wisdom, strengthens spells

Rue: protection, mental abilities, purification, health, comfort

Sage: healing, longevity, good health, psychic awareness, protection

St. John's Wort: courage, power of the sun, fertility, purification, healing, positive energy

Tarragon: cleansing, regeneration, transformation

Thyme: purification, psychic cleansing, divination, healing, enhances memory, eases sleep, courage

Valerian (all-heal): purification, protection, healing, love, sleep, attraction

Vanilla: love, prosperity, lust, energy, mental abilities, creativity

Verbena (vervain): purification, protection, blessings, communication with nature spirits

Violet: tranquility, love, luck, protection, healing

Walnut: healing, mental abilities

Willow: communication, eloquence, protection, healing, love, dreams

Yarrow: marriage, courage, love and friendship, psychic abilities, hex breaking